The Reformation of the sixteenth century was a movement which divided Christendom, destroyed the old medieval conception of society and laid the foundations of modern Europe. This book tells the story of that shattering upheaval in a unique way, by means of extracts from a large variety of contemporary writings—memoirs and diaries, songs and prayers, laws and reports, trials and confessions.

It begins with some of the weaknesses within the Medieval Church which prepared the way for the disaster it suffered. It tells of the two main branches of Protestantism on the Continent—Lutheranism and Calvinism—which were both deeply indebted to the personal experiences and beliefs of their founders and grew in different ways, and also of the Counter-Reformation which halted the spread of the new ideas.

Finally, a large part of the book is devoted to the English Reformation, which was inspired by events from abroad and yet contributed its own principles and developments to bring about one of the greatest revolutions in the country's history, one which did much to produce present-day English society.

Illustrated throughout with pictures drawn from contemporary sources, this addition to the WAYLAND DOCUMENTARY HISTORY SERIES offers an exciting and authentic approach to history studies.

Frontispiece Preaching at St Paul's Cross, London, during the sixteenth century

The Reformation
of the
Sixteenth Century

by Leonard W. Cowie

WAYLAND PUBLISHERS LONDON

In this series

THE BLACK DEATH AND PEASANTS' REVOLT   Leonard Cowie
MEDIEVAL PILGRIMS   Alan Kendall
PLAGUE AND FIRE   Leonard Cowie
THE REFORMATION OF THE SIXTEENTH CENTURY   Leonard Cowie

First published in 1970 by
Wayland (Publishers) Ltd
61 Western Road, Hove
East Sussex BN3 1JD, England

© Copyright 1972 Wayland (Publishers) Ltd

2nd Impression 1986

ISBN 0 85340 008 3

Printed and bound at
The Bath Press Avon, England

Contents

The Illustrations

1 Before the Reformation

MANY factors brought about the Reformation. It was realised in the Church that the clergy, from the bishops downwards, were failing in their duty. Educated people disliked the superstitions connected with pilgrimages, indulgences and other practices; and the restrictions on Bible-reading were resented. Huss foreshadowed the ideas of the Reformation, and Savonarola its moral austerity. The Popes acted as rich princes rather than as meek spiritual leaders. The invention of printing and the revival of learning during the Renaissance stimulated critics of the Church, the most notable of whom was Erasmus.

A preacher in Strasbourg Cathedral at the end of the fifteenth century foresaw the catastrophe threatening the Medieval Church: 'O Lord my God, how falsely now do even those live who seem most spiritual — Parsons and Monks, Béguines and Penitents! Their study is not to work God's works but to conceal the Devil's works. Among these all is outward show, and there is no truth, nought else but dung be-snowed or buried under snow; without is the glistering whiteness of righteousness and honesty, but within a conscience reeking with vermin and with the stench of sin. The day shall come when the Sun of Righteousness shall melt the snow, and then shall the secrets of your hearts be revealed. And would that the filth of our sins were at least covered with the appearance of snow, that our sin, like Sodom, were not published abroad without shame! (1).'

Many people were beginning to feel that all was not well with the Church. One problem involved confirmation. Since medieval bishops had no settled times or places for confirming, it was often complained that many people died unconfirmed. It was usual for

A prophecy

Confirmation

11

people to try to catch them on their way through a district as they did with St Anselm in France in the eleventh century: 'Anselm, therefore, set out from Wissant early on the morrow, and came after certain days to St Omer, where he was received with joy by clergy and monks, and detained for five days; during which time, at the prayer of the canons, he consecrated an altar. After which there came to him certain honourable men of those parts, kneeling at his feet and beseeching him to confirm their children by the laying on of hands and anointing with sacred oil. To whom he made answer forthwith: "Not only will I gladly receive those for whom ye pray in this matter, but others also who present themselves shall not be rejected." They, marvelling at the great man's benignity in so

German monks at worship

easy a condescension, were rejoiced above measure and gave him thanks; and, when their children had been confirmed, they forth-with filled the whole city with the words which they had received from his lips. Then might ye see men and women, great and small, pouring forth from their houses and outrunning each other in their haste to reach our lodging and share in so great a sacrament; for it was now many years since any bishop had suffered himself to be employed in any such office among them (2).'

A distinguished German monk wrote a book in 1493 in which he complained of the neglect of worship and learning among his fellow-monks: 'All is confusion, profanity, presumption. If we look to divine service, they perform this so confused and disorderly and dissolutely that there is no sound of sense in their words nor of due melody in their chants; for they lack all erudition in the liberal arts, so that they understand no whit of all that they sing; wherefore they not so much recite, as confound their canonical services, without either affection or devotion or savour of inward sweetness. Never are the Holy Scriptures seen in their hands, never do they do their duty in edifying discourse, never do they take account of training in morals (3).'

The monk and his greyhounds, from *The Canterbury Tales*

The neglect of the monks was matched by the superstition of the people. A French monk in the eleventh century described how popular superstition might lead to the creation of a saint and pilgrimages to his tomb: 'I have indeed seen, and blush to relate, how a common boy, nearly related to a certain most renowned abbot, and squire (it was said) to some knight, died in a village hard by Beauvais on Good Friday, two days before Easter. Then, for the sake of that sacred day whereon he had died, men began to

13

impute a gratuitous sanctity to the dead boy. When this had been rumoured among the country-folk, all agape for something new, then forthwith oblations and waxen tapers were brought to his tomb by villagers of all that country round. What need of more words? A monument was built over him, the spot was hedged in with a stone building, and from the very confines of Brittany there came great companies of country-folk, though without admixture of the higher sort (4).'

Three of Chaucer's Canterbury pilgrims, *left to right* the serjeant-at-law, the second nun, and the reeve

Miracles and frauds   Sir Thomas More told how a priest might stage fraudulent miracles to attract pilgrims and their offerings to his church: 'Some priest, to bring up a pilgrimage in his parish, may devise some false fellow feigning himself to come seek a saint in his church, and there suddenly say, that he hath gotten his sight. Then shall he have the bells rung for a miracle, and the fond folk of the country soon made fools, then women coming thither with their candles. And the person buying of some lame beggar, three or four pairs of their old crutches with twelve pence spent in men and women of wax thrust through divers places some with arrows, and some with rusty knives, will make his offerings for one seven years worth twice his tithes (5).'

Indulgences   Once the pilgrims had arrived, the priests frequently offered them indulgences or pardons for their sins. This was one of the many indulgences to be obtained at the Brigittine monastery of Syon at Isleworth in Middlesex: '*Item* In the Feast of St Bridget whosoever

14

will come to the said monastery, devoutly there visiting the Holy Virgin St Bridget, and giving some alms to the sustentation of the same monastery, shall have pardon and clean remission in all cases, reserved and unreserved, and this pardon endureth from the beginning of the first evensong till the last evensong be done (6).'

Yet, although indulgences and pardons were freely offered to the faithful, the Church insisted that the Bible be only available in Latin—a dead language that few ordinary people could read. Sir Thomas More, though a liberal and enlightened man, did not think that everyone should be allowed to read the Bible freely:

The half-closed Bible

Pilgrim badges, like these of Canterbury above, were a good source of revenue for priests at famous shrines

'Though the bishop might unto some layman betake and commit with good advice and instruction the whole Bible to read, yet might he to some man well and with reason restrain the reading of some part, and from some busybody the meddling with any part at all, more than he shall hear in sermons set out and declared unto him, and in like wise to take the Bible away from such folk again, as be proved by their blind presumption to abuse the occasion of their profit unto their own hurt and harm. And thus may the bishop order the scripture in our hands, with as good reason as the father doth by his discretion appoint which of his children may for his sadness keep a knife to cut his meat, and which shall for his wantonness have his knife taken from him for cutting of his fingers (7).'

John Huss of Bohemia was burned for his beliefs in 1415. Like many people, he felt that Christianity ought to be a religion of the people. Here are some of his statements, as recorded in Foxe's *Book of Martyrs:* 'False it is that they say the Pope and his cardinals

John Huss, early Protestant

15

to be the true and manifest successors of Peter and of the apostles, neither that any other successors of Peter and of the apostles can be found upon the earth besides them: whereas all bishops and priests be successors of Peter and of the apostles.

Not the Pope, but Christ only, is the head; and not the cardinals, but all Christ's faithful people, be the body of the Catholic Church.

If the Pope be a reprobate, it is plain that he is no head, no nor member even, of the Holy Church of God, but of the devil and of his synagogue.

Neither is it true, that we ought to stand in all things to the determination of the Pope and of the cardinals, but so far forth as they do agree with the holy Scripture of the Old and New Testament.

The Church of Rome is not that place where the Lord did appoint the principal see of His whole Church: for Christ, Who was the head priest of all, did first sit in Jerusalem, and Peter did sit first in Antioch, and afterward in Rome. Also other Popes did sit, some at Bologna, some at Perugia, some at Avignon (8).'

Savonarola, early Puritan
From 1494 to 1498 an Italian friar, Savonarola, directed a revival in Florence which foreshadowed much of the later results of the Reformation. He believed in good works by ordinary people: 'He achieved a holy and admirable work in his reforms of morals. There was never so much religion and virtue in Florence as in his day, and after his death the fall of piety and virtue was kept within limits. The taverns were closed, women dressed modestly, and children lived a life of holiness. Conducted by Fra Buonvincini they went in bands to church, wore their hair short and pelted with stones and insults gamblers, drunkards and women of immodest dress (9).'

A Renaissance Pope
The Renaissance Popes of the late fifteenth and early sixteenth centuries were corrupt and secular in outlook. Here is a shocking account of the election of Pope Alexander VI in 1492: 'To Innocent [VIII] succeeded Rodrigo Borgia of Valenza, a royal city in Spain. He was an ancient cardinal and made the best figure in Rome. His election was owing partly to the disputes that arose between the two cardinals, heads of factions, Ascanio Sforza and Giuliano of S. Pietro in Vincula, but chiefly to a simony unheard of in those days. For Borgia openly corrupted many of the cardinals, some with money, others with promises of profitable places and benefices, of which he had many at that time in his power; and they, without any

Facing page Florence in the sixteenth century

regard to the precepts of the Gospel, were not ashamed of making a traffic of the sacred treasures, under the name of Divine Authority, and that in the most high and eminent seat of the Christian religion (10).'

A soldier Pope

Pope Julius II in 1511 actually commanded a Papal Army, in the siege of an Italian town held by the French. This military behaviour greatly upset many people. 'It was certainly a remarkable case, and a sight very uncommon in the eye of the world ... to behold the High Priest, the Vicar of Christ on earth, old and infirm, and educated in ease and pleasures, now employed in person in managing a war excited by himself against Christians; and at the siege of a paltry town exposing himself to all the fatigues and dangers of a commander of armies, and retaining nothing of the Pontiff but the name and the habit (11).'

'In Praise of Folly'

A satirical attack on other ecclesiastical abuses was made in an extract from *In Praise of Folly* written in 1509 by the Dutch scholar, Erasmus: 'What shall I say of such as cry up and maintain the cheat of pardons and indulgences? that by these compute the time of each soul's residence in purgatory, and assign them a longer or shorter continuance, according as they purchase more or fewer of these paltry pardons and saleable exemptions? Or what can be said bad enough of others, who pretend that by force of such magical charms, or by the fumbling over their beads in the rehearsal of such and such petitions (which some religious imposters invented, either for diversion, or what is more likely for advantage), they shall procure riches, honour, pleasure, health, long life, a lusty old age, nay, after death a sitting at the right hand of our Saviour in His kingdom; though as to this last part of their happiness, they care not how long it be deferred, having scarce any appetite toward a-tasting the joys of heaven, till they are surfeited, glutted with, and can no longer relish their enjoyments on earth (12).'

2 *Luther: The Pope Defied*

THE REFORMATION really began when Martin Luther (1483–1546), a German friar and lecturer at the University of Wittenberg, criticised the idea of indulgences. He was unexpectedly driven by this action to challenge the whole position of the Pope's authority, and much of the teaching of the Medieval Church. The climax of his defiance came when he refused to give up his beliefs at the Diet of Worms, which was the supreme assembly of the Holy Roman Empire.

Luther always remembered vividly how, as a schoolboy, he had seen Prince William of Anhalt who had joined a Franciscan friary in Magdeburg: 'Once when on my way to school at Magdeburg at the time when I was fourteen, I saw the prince of Anhalt going barefoot and cowled in the public street, begging for bread and carrying the sack like a donkey. He looked the image of death, nothing but skin and bone; in fact, he died shortly afterwards, unable to stand such a rigorous life. Those who saw him were struck with awe and could not help being ashamed that they too were not friars (13).' *A princely friar*

Luther himself became a friar in 1505 and lived an austere and pious life, but could find no spiritual relief. For years he studied the Scriptures, especially St Paul's Epistles: 'I greatly longed to understand Paul's Epistle to the Romans and nothing stood in the way but that one expression, "the justice of God", because I took it to mean that justice whereby God is just and deals justly in punishing the unjust. My situation was that, although an impeccable friar, I stood before God as a sinner troubled in conscience, and I had no confidence that my merit would assuage him. Therefore I did not love a just and angry God, but rather hated and murmured against him. Yet I clung to the dear Paul and had a great yearning to know *The troubled friar* what he meant (14).'

Luther was urgently aware of the contrast between God's supreme goodness and man's desperate wickedness. He wrote: 'It is God's eternity, holiness and power which thus continuously threaten man throughout the whole of his life. God's ever-present judgment clutches man in the loneliness of his conscience, and with his every breath conveys him to the Almighty and Holy One to prosper or destroy (15).'

Luther finds peace At last in 1515, he found spiritual relief while studying the verse in St Paul's Epistle to the Romans, 'The just shall live by his faith': 'Night and day I pondered until I saw the connection between the justice of God and that statement that "the just shall live by his faith". Then I grasped that the justice of God is that righteousness by which through grace and sheer mercy God justifies us through faith. This immediately made me feel as if I had been born again and had entered paradise through newly opened doors. The whole of Scripture took on a new meaning, and whereas before the "justice of God" had filled me with hate, now it became to me inexpressibly sweet in greater love, so that the passage of Paul became to me a gate of heaven (16).'

Upon this experience Luther based his central doctrine of justification by faith, the idea that a Christian could enter the kingdom of Heaven by his beliefs alone: 'If you have a true faith that Christ is your Saviour, then at once you have a gracious God, for faith leads you in and opens up God's heart and will, that you should see pure grace and overflowing love. This it is to behold God in faith that you should look upon His fatherly, friendly heart, in which there is no anger nor ungraciousness. He who sees God as angry does not see Him rightly, but looks only on a curtain, as if a dark cloud had been drawn across his faith (17).'

Justification by faith Justification by faith, Luther insisted, meant that a man was free from human authority such as the Pope, and answerable to God alone: 'Faith is enough for a Christian, he does not need any works: he is definitely freed from all commandments and all laws, and if he is freed from them, he is surely free. Such is Christian liberty, and faith alone causes it (18).'

Certainty in religion To Luther the only certainty in religion was a man's own personal experience of God's truth: 'If our theology achieves certainty, it is because it takes us away from ourselves and puts us outside ourselves, so that we no longer rely on our own strength, our conscience, our senses, our personality, our works, but only on what is beyond ourselves, namely the promise and truth of God who cannot deceive us (19).'

He believed that a man must find his own salvation and not rely upon 'works' (baptism, confirmation and other outward actions): 'The freedom of conscience is that which frees our conscience from works, not in order to reject them completely, but in order to avoid putting our trust in them (20).'

Personal Salvation and scripture

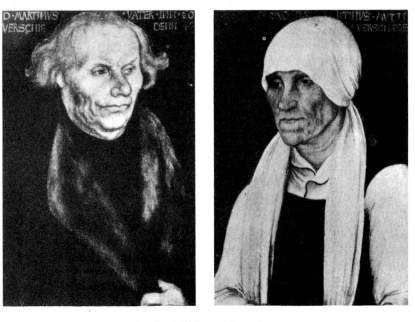

Luther's father and mother

Scripture alone, he urged, must guide a man in religion: 'The conscience must not be bound by anything except by the Word of God (21).'

Luther was aroused to action by the question of indulgences. The theory behind indulgences, as Pope Clement VI had stated in a Bull of 1343, was that the saints had handed down to the Church a 'treasury of merit' available for the pardon of sinners: 'And to this heap of treasure the merits of the blessed Mother of God and of all the

Indulgences

21

elect, from the first just man to the last, are known to have supplied their increment: and no diminution or washing away of this treasure is in any wise to be feared, as well because of the infinite merits of Christ (as aforesaid) as because the more men are drawn to righteousness as a result of its application by so much the more does the heap of merits increase. ... (22).'

Tetzel's campaign   In 1517 Pope Leo X commissioned John Tetzel, a Dominican friar, to sell thousands of pounds worth of indulgences in Germany to raise money for the rebuilding of the cathedral of St Peter's, Rome. This is an account by an eyewitness of his campaign: '[Tetzel] gained by his preaching in Germany an immense sum of money, all of which he sent to Rome: and especially at the new mining works at St Annaberg, where I, Frederick Mecum, heard him for two years, a large sum was collected. It is incredible what this ignorant and impudent friar gave out. He said that if a Christian had slept with his mother, and placed the sum of money in the Pope's indulgence chest, the Pope had power in heaven and earth to forgive the sin, and, if he forgave it, God must do so also. Item, if they contributed readily and bought grace and indulgence, all the hills of St Annaberg would become pure massive silver. Item, so soon as the coin rang in the chest, the soul for whom the money was paid would go straightway to heaven. The indulgence was so highly prized that, when the commissary entered a city, the Bull was borne on a satin or gold-embroidered cushion, and all the priests and monks, the town council, schoolmaster, scholars, men, women, maidens, and children, went out to meet him with banners and tapers, with songs and procession. Then all the bells were rung, all the organs played; he was conducted into the church, a red cross was erected in the midst of the church, and the Pope's banner displayed; in short, God himself could not have been welcomed and entertained with greater honour (23).'

The Ninety-five Theses (1517)   Luther was shocked. He nailed his *Ninety-Five Theses* on the door of Wittenberg Church. These are some extracts from a sermon on *Indulgence and Grace* in which he explained them to the people: 'Sixth, it cannot be proved from any Scripture that divine justice requires or desires any other punishment or satisfaction from the sinner than his hearty and true repentance and conversion, with a resolution henceforth to bear the cross of Christ and practise the

22

BULLÆ INDULGE[...]

Iohannes Tetzel von Leipzig
S.S. Theol. Doctor und Professor ein Brude[r]

good works before-mentioned, also imposed on him by no man ...

'Ninth, if the Church were at this day to decide and declare that indulgence made more satisfaction than works, still it were a thousand-fold better that no Christian man should purchase or desire the indulgence, but rather perform the works and suffer loss ...

'Fourteenth, indulgence is allowed for the sake of imperfect and slothful Christians, who will not exercise themselves industriously in good works or are impatient. For indulgence improves no man, but only tolerates and allows his imperfection. So men should not speak against indulgence, but neither should they persuade any one to take it (24).'

Luther was severely condemned for this in the Bull of Pope Leo X: 'We can no longer suffer the serpent to creep through the field of the Lord. The books of Martin Luther which contain these errors are to be examined and burned. As for Martin himself, good God, what office of paternal love have we omitted in order to recall him from his errors? Have we not offered him a safe conduct and money for the journey? And he has had the temerity to appeal to a future council, although our predecessors, Pius II and Julius II, subjected such appeals to the penalties of heresy. Now therefore we give Martin sixty days in which to submit, dating from the time of the publication of this Bull in his district. Anyone who presumes to infringe our excommunication and anathema will stand under the wrath of Almighty God and of the Apostles Peter and Paul (25).' But Luther ignored this. *Luther condemned (1520)*

In a letter to a friend he commented on the Bull: 'This Bull condemns Christ himself. It summons me not to an audience but to a recantation. I am going to act on the assumption it is spurious, though I think it is genuine. Would that Charles were a man and would fight for Christ against these Satans. But I am not afraid. God's will be done. I do not know what the prince should do unless to dissemble. I am sending you a copy of the Bull that you may see the Roman monster. The faith and the Church are at stake. I rejoice to suffer in so noble a cause. I am not worthy of so holy a trial. I feel much freer now that I am certain the pope is Antichrist (26).'

Luther had now moved on to attack the whole position of the Pope, as shown in this extract from an account by John Eck, a

Facing page Pope Leo X who condemned Luther

Professor of Theology, with whom Luther had a debate at Leipzig: 'Luther denies that Peter was the chief of the apostles: he declares that ecclesiastical obedience is not based on divine right, but that it was introduced by the ordinance of men or of the emperor. He denies that the Church was built upon Peter: "Upon this rock", etc. (27).'

Here is a sympathetic description by an eyewitness of Luther at Leipzig: 'Martin is of middle height, emaciated from care and study, so that you can almost count his bones through his skin. He is in the vigour of manhood and has a clear, penetrating voice. He is learned and has the Scripture at his fingers' ends. He knows Greek and Hebrew sufficiently to judge of the interpretations. A perfect forest of words and ideas stands at his command. He is affable and friendly, in no sense dour or arrogant. He is equal to anything. In company he is vivacious, jocose, always cheerful and gay no matter how hard his adversaries press him. Everyone chides him for the fault of being a little too insolent in his reproaches and more caustic than is prudent for an innovator in religion or becoming to a theologian (28).'

'Priesthood of
all believers' In an *Appeal to the German Nobility* in 1520, Luther put forward the doctrine of the priesthood of all believers: 'There has been a fiction by which the Pope, bishops, priests, and monks are called the "spiritual estate"; princes, lords, artisans and peasants are the "temporal estate". This is an artful lie and hypocritical invention, but let no one be made afraid by it, and that for this reason: that all Christians are truly of the spiritual estate, and there is no difference among them, save of office. As St Paul says (1 Cor. xii), we are all one body, though each member does its own work so as to serve the others. This is because we have one baptism, one Gospel, one faith, and are all Christians alike; for baptism, Gospel, and faith, these alone make spiritual and Christian people (29).'

The Diet of
Worms (1521) But storms gathered on the horizon. Luther was summoned to appear before the Diet of Worms and called upon to take back what he had said. He made this reply: 'Unless I am convicted of error by the testimony of Scripture or (since I put no trust in the unsupported authority of Pope or of councils, since it is plain that they have often erred and often contradicted themselves) by manifest reasoning I stand convicted by the Scriptures to which I have appealed, and

26

my conscience is taken captive by God's word, I cannot and will not recant anything, for to act against our conscience is neither safe for us, nor open to us. On this I take my stand. I can do no other. God help me. Amen (30).'

Charles V wrote angrily of Luther: 'A single monk, led astray by private judgement, has set himself against the faith held by all Christians for a thousand years and more, and impudently concludes that all Christians up till now have erred. I have therefore resolved to stake upon this cause all my dominions, my friends, my body and my blood, my life and soul. For myself and you, sprung from the holy German nation, appointed by peculiar privilege defenders of the faith, it would be a grievous disgrace, an eternal stain upon ourselves and posterity, if, in this our day, not only

Luther testifying before the Diet of Worms

heresy, but its very suspicion, were due to our neglect. After Luther's stiff-necked reply in my presence yesterday, I now repent that I have so long delayed proceedings against him and his false doctrines. I have now resolved never again, under any circumstances, to hear him (31).'

Albert Dürer

But Albert Dürer, the artist, greatly admired Luther and wrote in his diary: 'Every man who reads Luther's books may see how clear and transparent is his doctrine, because he sets forth the holy Gospel. Wherefore his books are to be held in great honour and not to be burnt; unless indeed his adversaries, who ever strive against the truth and would make gods out of men, were also cast into the fire, they and all their opinions with them, and afterwards a new edition of Luther's works were prepared. Oh God, if Luther be dead, who will henceforth expound to us the holy Gospel with such clearness. What, oh God, might he not still have written for us in ten or twenty years! (32).'

Support for Luther

An extract from a despatch from the Venetian Ambassador to the Diet, shows how much German opinion favoured Luther: 'Luther is a man who will not relinquish his opinion, either through argument, fear or entreaty ... He has many powerful partisans who encourage him, and against whom none dares to proceed ... His books are sold publicly in Worms, although the Pope and the Emperor, who is on the spot, have prohibited them (33).'

3 Luther: The New Church Established

ALTHOUGH he had not intended it, the result of Luther's defiance of the Pope was the birth of a separate Lutheran Church which became popular in many parts of Germany. It developed its own beliefs, expressed in Luther's Catechism and the Confession of Augsburg, and its own form of worship for which Luther wrote hymns. Luther himself was moderate in his religious outlook and would not support the revolutionary hopes of the German peasants. He married, and led a happy family life. Though he was influential outside Germany, his reliance upon the German princes to forward his movement restricted the spread of Lutheranism abroad, and after his death the Peace of Augsburg split Germany between the new and old religions.

A papal envoy reported on Nuremberg, a Lutheran town, in 1524: *A Lutheran*
'We arrived at Nuremberg on the Wednesday in Passion Week. In *town*
these parts the sincere faith of Christ is utterly cancelled; no respect is paid either to the Virgin Mary or the saints. On the contrary, it is said that those who employ their aid sin mortally. They deride the Papal rights and call the relics of the saints bones of those who have been hanged. In Lent they eat meat openly, saying they do not consider it prohibited. Confession is neglected, as they say it should be made to God, and that auricular confession is a buffoonery. They generally communicate under both forms. They make a laughing-stock of the Pope and Cardinals, and other ambassadorial ecclesiastics, by means of paintings and other caricatures. In short, they consider Martin their illuminator, and that until now they have been in darkness, and the indulgences are held by them like bread sold in the market-place (34).'

Here is an account by a Yorkshire seaman, who was at Bremen in 1528, of the new services there: 'And there the people did follow Luther's works and no masses were said there, but on the Sunday the priest would revest himself and go to the altar, and proceeded till nigh the sacring time [consecration of the bread and wine], and then the priest and all that were in the church, old and young, would sing after their mother tongue and there was no sacring (35).'

Luther seeks unity In 1522, Luther had to urge moderation upon his followers in a sermon in Wittenberg Church, so as to preserve unity: 'What you did was good, but you have gone too fast, for there are brothers and sisters on the other side who belong to us and must still be won. ...Faith never yields, but love is guided according as to how our neighbours can grasp or follow it. There are some who can run, others must walk, and still others who can hardly creep. Therefore we must not look on our own, but on our brother's powers, so that he that is weak in faith ... may not be destroyed ... Let us therefore throw ourselves at one another's feet, join hands and help one another (36).'

Anabaptists In the climate of new thinking, some people joined the Anabaptists, a sect which opposed infant baptism. One of them explained their views in a letter of 1524: 'We believe ... that all children who have not yet come to know the difference between good and evil ... are saved by the sufferings of Christ ... Also that infant baptism is a silly blasphemous outrage, contrary to all Scripture ... Since ... you have published your protestations against infant baptism, we hope you do not act against the eternal Word, wisdom, and command of God, according to which only believers should be baptized, and that you baptize no children (37).'

Peasants' Revolt (1524) Social disorder soon followed in the wake of religious turbulence. When the Peasants' Revolt first broke out in Germany in 1524, Luther condemned the landowners, saying: 'They can hardly do anything else than flay and beat and add one burden upon another. Now God is going to punish them by rebellion of the oppressed. They ought not, they cannot, they will not endure your tyranny and insolence any longer. No longer is the world in such a state that you can please yourself how you drive and hunt human beings. Therefore let the Word of God do its work (38).'

But he was alarmed when the peasants claimed that he supported *their* demands; and he warned them: 'If you are anxious to appeal to the rights laid down by the Gospel, then remember that these rights consist in suffering with Christ on the Cross (39).'

And, as the violence of the peasants increased, he wrote a strong pamphlet, *Against the Murdering, Thieving Hordes of the Peasants,* saying: 'If the peasant is in open rebellion, then he is outside the law of God, for rebellion is not simply murder, but it is like a great fire which attacks and lays waste a whole land. Thus, rebellion brings with it a land full of murders and bloodshed, makes widows and orphans and turns everything upside-down like a great disaster. Therefore, let everyone who can, smite, slay and stab, secretly or openly, remembering that nothing can be more poisonous, hurtful or devilish than a rebel. It is just as when you must kill a mad dog; if you don't strike, he will strike you and the whole land with you (40).'

In the following years, Luther worked to provide instruction for his own Church people. This extract from his *Short Catechism* (1529) explains the meaning of the first sentence of the Creed, 'I believe in God the Father Almighty, Maker of heaven and earth': 'I believe that God has created me and all other creatures, and has given me, and preserves for me, body and soul, eyes, ears, and all my limbs, my reason and all my senses; and that daily He bestows on me clothes and shoes, meat and drink, house and home, wife and child, fields and cattle, and all my goods, and supplies in abundance all needs and necessities of my body and life, and protects me from all perils, and guards and defends me from all evil. And this He does out of pure fatherly and Divine goodness and mercy, without any merit or worthiness in me; for all which I am bound to thank Him and praise Him, and, moreover, to serve and obey Him. This is a faithful saying (41).'

To those who thought the Catechism was too slight and short, he replied: 'Do not think the Catechism is a little thing to be read hastily and cast aside. Although I am a doctor, I have to do just as a child and say word for word every morning and whenever I have time the Lord's Prayer and the Ten Commandments, the Creed and the Psalms. I have to do it every day, and yet I cannot understand as I would. But these smart folk in one reading want to be doctors of doctors. Therefore I beg these wise saints to be persuaded that they

Short Catechism (1529)

32

Martin Luther

are not such great doctors as they think. To be occupied with God's Word helps against the world, the flesh and the devil and all bad thoughts. This is the true holy water with which to exorcize the devil (42).'

These are two of the sections of the 'Confession of Augsburg' (1530), a statement of Lutheran belief written by Luther's friend, Philip Melanchthon: ' *Section Four: Of Justification*. They teach that men cannot be justified in the sight of God by their own strength, merits or works, but that they are justified freely on account of Christ through faith, when they believe that they are received into grace and that their sins are remitted on account of Christ who made satisfaction for sins on our behalf by his death. God imputes this faith for righteousness in his own sight (Romans iii and iv). *Confession of Augsburg (1530)*

Philip Melanchthon

'*Section Seven: Of the Church*. They teach that the one Holy Church will remain for ever. Now this Church is the congregation of the saints, in which the Gospel is rightly taught and the sacraments rightly administered. And for that true unity of the Church it is enough to have unity of belief concerning the teaching of the Gospel and the administration of the sacraments. It is not necessary

33

that there should everywhere be the same traditions of men, or the same rites and ceremonies devised by men … (43).'

The Confession of Augsburg was drawn up in a vain attempt to secure religious peace in Germany. Luther defended it against those who thought it was too conciliatory: 'I have been through our friend Philip's apologia, and it seems to me quite excellent. I should be at a loss to know how to alter or improve it. Nor should I be willing to try, because it is impossible for me to speak so gently or cautiously. May Christ our Lord grant that it will bear much rich fruit, as we all hope and pray. Amen (44).'

A Lutheran priest

Luther's hymns   Luther brought congregational singing into worship for the first time, because he greatly loved music: 'Experience proves that next to the Word of God only music deserves to be extolled as the mistress and governess of the feelings of the human heart. We know that to the devils music is distasteful and insufferable. My heart bubbles up and overflows in response to music, which has so often refreshed me from dire plagues (45).'

Here is a chronicler's account of an incident in the city of Magdeburg, concerning Luther's newfangled hymns: 'On the day of St

John between Easter and Pentecost, an old man, a weaver, came through the city gate to the monument of Emperor Otto and there offered hymns for sale while he sang them to the people. The burgomaster, coming from early mass and seeing the crowd, asked one of his servants what was going on. "There is an old rogue over there", he answered, "who is singing and selling the hymns of the heretic Luther". The burgomaster had him arrested and thrown into prison; but two hundred citizens interceded and he was released (46).'

Luther wrote thirty-six hymns. This is the first verse of his best-known:

> *A safe stronghold our God is still,*
> *A trusty shield and weapon;*
> *He'll help us clear from all the ill*
> *That hath us now o'ertaken.*
> *The ancient Prince of Hell*
> *Hath risen with purpose fell;*
> *Strong mail of Craft and Power*
> *He weareth in this hour,*
> *On earth is not his fellow (47).*

By way of contrast, here is the last verse of a Christmas hymn written by Luther for his little son Hans, in 1540:

> *Were earth a thousand times as fair*
> *Beset with gold and jewels rare,*
> *She yet were far too poor to be*
> *A narrow cradle, Lord, for Thee (48).*

Luther's house attracted crowds of followers and sightseers. A picture of Luther's crowded home is recounted in a letter to Prince George of Anhalt. The writer advises him not to spend a night there: 'The house of Luther is occupied by a motley crowd of boys, students, girls, widows, old women and youngsters. For this reason there is much disturbance in the place, and many regret it for the sake of the good man, the honourable father. If only the spirit of Doctor Luther lived in all of these, his house would offer you an agreeable, friendly quarter for a few days so that your Grace would be able to enjoy the hospitality of that man. But as the situation now stands and as circumstances exist in the household of Luther, I would not advise your Grace to stay there (49).'

Luther at home

35

Yet while Luther talked during these crowded meals, many made a note of what he said. A book was later published, called *Luther's Table Talk*. These are a few of his sayings from it: 'Printing is God's latest and best work to spread the true religion throughout the world—A dog is a most faithful animal and would be more highly prized if less common—They are trying to make me into a fixed star. I am an irregular planet—Germany is the pope's pig. That is why we have to give him so much bacon and sausages (50).'

In later life Luther fully enjoyed his meals, because: 'If our Lord found it right to create great pike and Rhenish wine, then we may take and use them (51).'

Luther at Wittenberg   As Luther's reputation grew, students from many countries came to Wittenberg to hear him teach. A contemporary said: 'As they came in sight of the town, they returned thanks to God with clasped hands, for from Wittenberg as heretofore from Jerusalem the light of evangelical truth hath spread to the utmost parts of the earth (52).'

France   Here is a letter written by Francis I in 1530; but in France, as elsewhere outside Germany, Lutheranism had little influence compared with Calvinism: 'We are much annoyed and displeased because this cursed heretical sect of Lutherans flourishes in our good city of Paris, the head and capital of our realm, containing the principal University of Christendom, where many will be able to imitate it. This sect we intend to attack with all our power and authority, sparing nobody. We therefore will and intend that such and so heavy punishment may fall upon it as to correct the cursed heretics and be an example to all others (53).'

Luther's last words   Two days before he died in 1546 Luther had inscribed a friend's book with a text from St John's Gospel, 'If anyone obeys my teaching, he shall never know what it is to die.' He added: 'How incredible is such a text, and yet it is the truth. If a man takes God's word in full earnest and believes in it and then falls asleep, he slips away without noticing death and is safe on the other side (54).'

The Peace of Augsburg (1555)   Lutheranism had become such a great movement, that a compromise agreement was adopted by the German princes in the Diet, letting each prince decide whether Lutheranism or Roman Catholicism should prevail in his state: 'In order to bring peace into the holy empire of the Germanic Nation, between the Roman Imperial Majesty and the Electors, Princes, and Estates: let neither his

Imperial Majesty nor the Electors, Princes, etc., do any violence or harm to any estate of the Empire on account of the Augsburg Confession, but let them enjoy their religious belief, liturgy and ceremonies as well as their estates and other rights and privileges in peace; and complete religious peace shall be obtained only by Christian means of amity, or under threat of the punishment of the imperial ban (55).'

HULRICHUS

Helveticus Ecclesiæ Tigur Pastor. Naf. Zugij, an 1493. Cujus ab hostib. xi. octob. an. 1531.

Zwinglius & calamo & sigms dum pugnat
Victo & vincenti par data palma fuit.

4 Calvinism in Switzerland

THE SWISS Reformation began in Zürich under Ulrich Zwingli (1484–1531). Zwingli was a radical reformer, unable to come to terms with Luther. After Zwingli's death, the leadership of the Swiss Reformation passed to John Calvin (1509–64), a Frenchman who developed his own form of Protestantism and made Geneva a very influential religious centre. His ideas inspired men in several countries, including the Presbyterians in Scotland and the Puritans in England.

Here is an extract from 'a history of the Reformation in Switzer- *The Swiss* land' written by Henry Bullinger, Zwingli's son-in-law and succes- *Clergy* sor as the Protestant leader in Zurich: 'At one time during these years, when all the deacons of the Confederation were assembled together, there were found not over three who were well read in the Bible. The others acknowledged that none of them had read even the New Testament, whereby we may understand how it was with the other clergy, with whom the case was still worse. For among the clergy there was almost no studying, but their exercise was in gaming, in feeding and in the practice of all luxuries. The more earnest were accused of hypocrisy. Those who studied somewhat devoted themselves to scholastic theology and canon law. The greater part preached out of sermon books, learning by heart sermons written by monks and printed, repeating them to the people without judgement ... (56).'

Another extract from Bullinger's history states: 'In the churches the mass had become a market and a place for bargaining; in fact, all sacraments and all things which one holds holy became venal and corrupt. The singing in parishes and monasteries was for the

39

most part superstitious, and the monasteries had fallen into all sorts of scandals and idolatries, where no one of them observed so much as the first of its own rules, let alone God's Word. Every day new altars, endowments, and endless numbers of idolatrous pilgrimages were established, to the great pleasure of the clergy, who threw into their bottomless sacks all that the common man as well as the noble possessed. Whereupon there was great complaint on all sides (57).'

The Colloquy of Marburg (1529)

Zwingli and Luther met for a general discussion at Marburg Castle, but, as Melanchthon reported, they failed to agree: 'At the end of the debate the Swiss asked that Luther would take them for brethren. This Dr Martin would not at all agree to. He even addressed them very seriously, saying that he was exceedingly surprised that they should regard him as a brother if they seriously believed their own doctrine true. But that was an indication that they themselves did not think there was much involved in the matter (58).'

Luther and Zwingli

The disagreement, as Luther explained, was about whether Christ was truly present in the Communion service: 'They professed with many words that they wished to agree with us so far as to say that the body of Christ is truly present in the Supper, but spiritually, with the sole view that we deign to call them brethren, and so feign harmony. This Zwingli begged with tears in his eyes before the Landgrave and all of them, saying, "There are no people on earth with whom I would rather be in harmony than with the Wittenburgers". They strove with the utmost eagerness and vigour to seem in harmony with us, and could never endure the expression I used, "You have a different spirit from ours". They burst into flame every time they heard it (59).'

The student Calvin

John Calvin was to become a great figure in the Reformation. He studied first theology and then law at French universities. He wrote in his *Commentary on the Psalms:* 'Ever since I was a child, my father had intended me for theology; but ... as he considered that the study of the law commonly enriched those who followed it, this expectation made him incontinently change his mind. That is why I was withdrawn from the study of philosophy and put to the study of the law, to which I strove to devote myself faithfully in obedience to my father. God, however, in his hidden providence, at last made me turn in another direction (60).'

Calvin described his conversion to Protestantism, which took place in 1533: 'The more closely I considered myself, the more my conscience was pricked with sharp goadings; so much that no other relief or comfort remained to me except to deceive myself by forgetting. But since nothing better offered itself, I went on still in the way I had begun: then, however, there arose quite another form of teaching, not to turn away from the profession of Christianity but to reduce it to its own source, and to restore it, as it were, cleansed from all filthiness to its own purity. But I, offended by this novelty, could hardly listen to it willingly; and must confess that at first I valiantly and bravely resisted. For since men are naturally obstinate and opinionated to maintain the institutions they have once received, it irked me much to confess that I had been fed upon error and ignorance all my life. One thing especially there was that prevented me from believing in those people, and that was reverence for the Church. But after I had listened for some time with open ears and suffered myself to be taught, I saw very well that such a fear, that the majesty of the Church might be diminished, was vain and superfluous (61).'

A letter, written in 1570 by the minister of the French congregation in London, speaks highly of Calvin: 'When I look back upon his frankness and integrity, his affectionate benevolence towards me and the familiar intimacy which I enjoyed for sixteen years, I cannot but grieve for my separation from such a friend, or, I would say, such a father. What labours, watchings and anxieties did he endure! With what wisdom and perspicacity did he foresee all dangers and how skilfully did he go out to meet them! No words of mine can declare the fidelity and prudence with which he gave counsel, the kindness with which he received all who came to him, the cleverness and promptitude with which he replied to those who asked for his opinion on the most important questions, and the ability with which he disentangled the difficulties and problems which were laid before him. Nor can I express the gentleness with which he would console the afflicted and raise the fallen and distressed, or his courage in adversity and moderation in prosperity (62).'

Here is an extract from Calvin's great book, the *Institutes of the* *Christian Religion*, talking about his doctrine of 'predestination', the idea that God has planned everything for each individual:

'In conformity to the clear teaching of scripture we assert by an eternal and immutable counsel God hath once for all determined both whom He would admit to salvation and whom He would condemn to destruction. We affirm that this counsel, as far as concerns the elect, is founded on His gratuitous mercy, totally irrespective of human merit; but that to those whom He devotes to condemnation the gate of life is closed by a just and irreprehensible and incomprehensible judgement (63).'

Original sin

Calvin based his doctrine of predestination on man's complete sinfulness, which made it impossible for him to earn his salvation: 'Therefore original sin is seen to be an hereditary depravity and corruption of our nature, diffused into all parts of the soul ... wherefore those who have defined original sin as the lack of the original righteousness with which we should have been endowed, no doubt include, by implication, the whole fact of the matter, but they have not fully expressed the positive energy of this sin. For our nature is not merely bereft of good, but is so productive of every kind of evil that it cannot be inactive (64).'

Calvin and Servetus

A letter written from Calvin to his friend, John Farel, early in 1553, portrays his feelings about letters written to him by Michael Servetus. Servetus, a Spaniard, denied the divinity of Christ and later that year went to Geneva, where he was burned at the stake for heresy: 'Servetus recently wrote to me and has joined to his correspondence a long volume full of his mad ideas, adding with theatrical pomposity that I would see in that book some astounding and until then unheard of things. If I like, he will come here. But I do not want to bind myself. Because if he came, and my authority still counted for something, I would never let him leave alive (65).'

Servetus himself, however, believed that obstinate heretics should be put to death, as he explained in this letter to Calvin: 'It is God's truth that the severity of the death penalty was relaxed with the coming of Jesus Christ, if and when there is hope of amendment ... It is true that St Peter punished with death Ananias and Saphira, of whom he had no hope of conversion, to show more clearly his detestation of their crime, and to make them examples for all others, or because the Holy Spirit, whom they had scorned, made plain by that measure that they were incorrigible and obdurate in their wrong. This crime simply deserves death both before God and man. As to other crimes about which the Spirit has not laid down anything particular, where the evil has not taken root, and where one cannot point to deliberate obstinacy or an altogether monstrous wickedness, we should rather hope for correction by other punishments than death. Among such punishments banishment is praiseworthy as it is approved by Jesus Christ as excommunication is approved by the Church (66).'

In 1554 Melanchthon wrote to Calvin: 'I have read the writing *Melanchthon* in which you have refuted the detestable blasphemies of Servetus, and I return thanks to the Son of God who was the arbiter of your combat. To you also, the Church owes, and will in the future owe, gratitude. I am in entire agreement with your judgment. I affirm also that your Magistracy has acted justly in putting this blasphemer to death after a regular trial (67).'

Calvin stated in his *Institutes* that the government he preferred *Calvin and* was an aristocracy, by which he meant control of the State by *politics* godly people: 'I, for my part, am far from denying that the form which greatly surpasses the others is aristocracy, either pure or modified by popular government ... This has already been proved by experience and confirmed also by the authority of the Lord himself, when he established an aristocracy bordering on popular government among the Israelites, keeping them under that as the best form until he exhibited an image of the Messiah in David (68).'

Calvin insisted that subjects had no right to disobey their rulers: 'We must subject ourselves and be obedient to whatever superiors are ruling in the place where we are living (69).'

In his *Institutes*, Calvin expressed his idea of the duty of the State in religious matters: 'The State exists in order that idolatry, blasphemy of the Name of God and against His truth and other scandals to religion, be not publicly set forth and broadcast among the people; that public peace be not troubled, that each be secured in what is his own, that men's intercourse may be without fraud and violence, in fine that among Christians there may be some public and visible form of religion and that humanity be settled among men (70).'

Calvin describes the ideal Church in his *Institutes*: 'Above all *Calvin's ideal* where we see the word of God to be purely preached and listened *Church* to, the Sacraments administered according to the institution by Christ, there without any shadow of doubt is the Church ... The

43

Church universal is the whole body of people who accept the truth of God and the doctrine of His word, however diverse be their nationalities ... Under this universal Church, the Churches which are distributed throughout every town and village are thus reckoned, each of them, to have the title and authority of Church (71).'

In 1541 Calvin laid down that there were four ministries in his Church. These were: those who cared for the congregation, those who taught, those who organised, and those who gave out the alms: 'There are four orders of offices that our Lord instituted for the government of his Church: first the pastors, then the teachers, after them the elders, and fourthly the deacons (72).'

Geneva   A passage in the *Institutes* foretold how Calvin and his followers would rule Geneva: 'Administration is to know that by the word of God boldly they dare anything and compel all glory, boldness and virtue in this world to obey and to yield to the divine majesty; that by this word they are given commandment over the whole world to build up the house of Christ and to demolish the rule of Satan; to feed the sheep and to kill the wolves: to guide by instruction and exhortation the tractable: to constrain and correct the rebellious and self-willed: to bind and unbind: to thunder and lighten: but always in the word of God (73).'

In 1541 the General Council of the people of Geneva adopted Calvin's idea of the organisation of the Church, by laying down in the preamble to the Ordinances: 'It has seemed good to us that the spiritual government, such as our Lord demonstrates and institutes it by his word, should be set down in good form, to take place and be observed among us. And thus have we ordered and established, to obey and to maintain in our town and territory the Ecclesiastical policy, which follows, as we see it is taken, from the Gospel of Jesus Christ (74).'

An Irishman   Geneva under Calvin impressed John Bale, an Irish bishop:
in Geneva   'Geneva seemeth to me to be the wonderful miracle of the whole world: so many from all countries come hither, as it were in a sanctuary, not to gather riches, but to live in poverty ... Is it not wonderful that Spaniards, Italians, Scots, Englishmen, Frenchmen, Germans, disagreeing in manners, speech, and apparel, sheeps and wolves, bulls and bears, being coupled with the only yoke of Christ, should live so lovingly and friendly, and that monks, laymen and

44

nuns disagreeing both in life and sect, should dwell together, like a spiritual and Christian congregation (75).'

John Knox, the Scottish reformer, was another fervent admirer of Calvin's Geneva: 'Geneva, where I neither fear man nor am ashamed to say that this is the most perfect school of Christ that ever was in the earth since the days of the apostles. In other places, I confess Christ to be truly preached; but manners and religion to be so sincerely reformed, I have not yet seen in any other place (76).'

Knox and Geneva

John Knox

PROMPTE ET SINCERE ·

IOHANNES · CALVINVS ·
ANNO · ÆTATIS ·53·
· B ·

46

John Calvin

5 Calvinism in France and the Netherlands

THE TWO most important Continental countries into which Calvinism spread were France and the Netherlands. In France it gained considerable support, but became involved in the struggle among the nobility to gain control of the throne. The result was the Massacre of St Bartholomew, and a long civil war in which Philip II of Spain supported the Roman Catholics. Eventually Calvinism was tolerated, but did not win over the French people.

The people of the Netherlands accepted Calvinism at the time when they were contending for their independence against Spain; and William of Orange became the leader and symbol of their struggle. He was assassinated, but the Dutch people were to win political and religious freedom by the end of the century.

Here is a report to the Venetian Ambassador in France, written in 1561. By this time the Huguenots (French Calvinists) had become widespread and very strong: 'Unless it otherwise pleases the Almighty, religious affairs will soon be in an evil case in France, because there is not one single province uncontaminated. Indeed, in some provinces, such as Normandy, almost the whole of Brittany, Touraine, Poitou, Gascony, and a great part of Languedoc, of Dauphiny and of Provence, comprising three fourths of the kingdom, congregations and meetings, which they call assemblies, are held; and in these assemblies they read and preach, according to the rites and usages of Geneva, without any respect either for the ministers of the king or the commandments of the king himself. This contagion has penetrated so deeply that it affects every class of persons, and, what appears more strange, even the ecclesiastical body itself. I do not mean only priests, friars and nuns, but even

France

47

bishops and many of the principal prelates, who hitherto had not shown any such disposition; and it is only on account of the rigorous execution of the law that other persons besides the populace have not disclosed themselves, because they have restrained themselves for the time being, from fear of the loss of their property and lives (77).'

Calvin's influence The same writer comments drily on the influence of Calvin himself in France: 'Your Serenity will hardly believe the influence which the principal minister of Geneva, by name Calvin, a Frenchman and a native of Picardy, possesses in this kingdom; he is a man of extraordinary authority, who by his mode of life, his doctrines, and his writings, rises superior to all the rest; and it is almost impossible to believe the enormous sums of money which are secretly sent to him from France to maintain his power (78).'

An uncertain future Finally, the Ambassador looked anxiously into the future of religion in France: 'It is sufficient to add that if God does not interfere, there is great and imminent danger that one of two things will happen in this kingdom: either that the truce, which is desired and sought publicly, will end by the heretics having churches wherein they can preach, read and perform their rites according to their doctrine, without hindrance and in like manner as they obtained their churches by command of the late king, given at Fontainebleau at the end of August, in compliance with a petition presented to him by the Admiral; or else that we shall see an obedience to the Pope and to the Catholic rites enforced, and shall have resort to violence and imbrue our hands in noble blood. For these reasons I foresee a manifest and certain division in the kingdom and civil war as a consequence; and this will be the cause of ruin both of the kingdom and of religion, because upon a change in religion a change in the state necessarily follows (79).'

Huguenot strictness An account was given by a Swiss traveller of the strictness of Huguenot discipline: 'Control of the Protestant faith is very severe. Anyone who attends mass, even once, is made to confess before the whole congregation, as if he had always been a papist, and he must ask to be reconciled. Those who have been denied communion, on account of some grave sin, are also compelled to appear before the whole assembly, if they wish to have grace, and if they do not do this, the communion is refused to them. Holy communion takes place only four times a year, at Christmas, at Easter, at Pentecost, and in September, and this makes it easy to exclude those who have been excommunicated (80).'

The same traveller describes the Communion services at Montpellier, a Huguenot stronghold: 'So that everyone may communicate the same morning the service begins two or three hours before daybreak. Immediately after the sermon the communion begins, during which some chapters of the New Testament are read from the pulpit. When the men, and afterwards the women, have communicated, a grace is said, the congregation sings, and then about seven o'clock everyone leaves the church. Immediately a second congregation enters, the singing begins again, then the sermon, and then communion, as before. This goes on sometimes until eleven o'clock or midday. Sometimes at Montpelier four to six thousand people communicate in a single day, and the crush is such that in winter the church is as warm as if it were heated (81).' *Huguenot worship*

A friend of Admiral Coligny, the leader of the French Huguenots, wrote in his biography of Coligny: 'When the time of the Lord's Supper was at hand, he was wont to call his domestics, and members of his household about him and make known unto them that he had to render an account unto God, not only of his own mode of life but of theirs. If any discord had fallen among them, they were reconciled. If any man seemed insufficiently prepared for the understanding and veneration of that great mystery, he caused him to be more diligently instructed in religion. If any seemed more stubborn, he told them openly that he would rather be alone in his house than keep a following of the wicked ... (83).' *Admiral Coligny*

A friend of Calvin observed in a letter to him written in 1562, the year the Wars of Religion broke out in France: 'Nothing disturbs us more than the baseness of the Church, not to give it a harder name. I have been as far as Angers, in peril of my life, but I was able to do little or nothing. Their violence in the destruction of altars is incredible, and we have been quite unable to prevent it here. In short, all things are suddenly changed, so that I am amazed at the spectacle; for the enemy in a hundred years, even if victorious, could not restore, in this one city alone, what has been destroyed in the space of two hours (84).' *Huguenot violence*

A French writer remarked sadly during the Wars of Religion:

'It would be impossible to tell you what barbarous cruelties are committed by both sides. Where the Huguenot is master, he ruins the images and demolishes the sepulchres and tombs. On the other hand, the Catholic kills, murders, and drowns all those whom he knows to be of that sect, until the rivers overflow with them (84).'

'Incredible obstinacy'

In 1569 an Englishman thought that the hatred of each side for the other during the wars was growing worse: 'And that withal the dreadfullest cruelties at once of the world, plague, hunger, and the sword, which God of his goodness cease in them and preserve from us; and to this is joined an incredible obstinacy of either side, even hardening their hearts with malice and fury to the utter extermination one of another (85).'

Massacre of St Bartholomew (1572)

In the end, some 15,000 Huguenots, including Coligny, were slaughtered in France in 1572. The thirteen year old Duke of Sully, later to be Henry IV's great minister, was one of the few Huguenots to escape in Paris: 'I put on my student's gown and, taking a large breviary under my arm, went downstairs. As I walked out into the street I was horrified; there were madmen running to and fro, smashing down doors and shouting, "Kill, kill, massacre the Huguenots". Blood spattered before my eyes and doubled my fear. I ran into a clump of soldiers, who stopped me. They plied me with questions and began to jostle me about when luckily they saw my breviary. That served as my safe conduct. Twice again the same thing happened and twice again I escaped (86).'

About the day the news of the Massacre of St Bartholomew reached Rome, a Cardinal reported: 'On the same morning ... his Holiness with the whole College of Cardinals went to the church of St Mark to have the *Te Deum* sung and to thank God for granting so great a favour to the Christian people. His Holiness does not cease to pray God, and to make others pray, to inspire the Most Christian King to follow further the path which he has opened and to cleanse and purge completely the Kingdom of France from the plague of the Huguenots. Also, this morning, His Holiness went in procession to the church of St Louis, where a solemn Mass was held with the same intention, and next week he will proclaim a solemn jubilee ... (87).'

Catherine de' Medici

A defence was given to the French Ambassador in Venice by the Queen Mother, Catherine de' Medici, who had made her son,

Facing page The Massacre of St Bartholomew

Charles IX, have the Huguenot leaders killed: 'I am certain it will be said that my son the King has only acted within his rights as a sovereign prince, and that the Admiral, strong and powerful as he was in this realm, could not otherwise be punished for his rebellion and disobedience but in the manner after which he and his party have been treated. The King is greatly troubled that in the heat of

Charles IX of France

the moment certain others of the religion were slain by the Catholics, who called to mind infinite evils, robberies and other wicked acts committed upon them during the troubles; but now at last all is peaceful, so that there is recognised only one King, and one justice rendered to all alike according to duty and equity, since the King is resolved, in view of the evils caused by the diversity of religions, to suffer none but his own (88).'

53

Facing page Admiral Coligny wounded during the Massacre of St Bartholomew. *Overleaf (pages 54–55)* Contemporary engraving of the day of the Massacre

Tilligny.

Der Admiral.

Der Admiral.

In 1589, however, the Huguenot leader Henry of Navarre became King of France as Henry IV, and the next year virtually ended the Wars of Religion by starving Paris into submission. An entry in a contemporary diary shortly before the end of the siege states: 'Monday, August 6 ... Over the portals of the butcher shops, where there are only pieces of old cow, mule, and cat, instead of the usual beef and mutton, I found the following written in capital letters. "These are the rewards of those who pour out their lifeblood for Philip" [Philip II of Spain] (89).'

A discussion took place between the Roman Catholic clergy and Henry of Navarre, who accepted Roman Catholicism on becoming King of France: 'When they came to the prayer for the dead, he said, "Let's skip the Requiem, I'm not dead yet and don't want to be". As for Purgatory, he said he believed in it, not as an article of faith, but as a doctrine of the Church, which he believed as a good son of the Church. He said this to please them, as it was their bread and butter. On the adoration of the sacrament, "You haven't satisfied me on this point ... but look here: today I put my soul in your hands. I beg you take good care of it. Where I go in today I will not come out till death, I swear and protest to you". As he said this, there were tears in his eyes ... (90).'

This report was given by a Parisian of the time: 'A bishop said to a friend of mine, on the same subject, "I am a Catholic by life and profession and a faithful servant of the King. I will live and die as such. But I think it would have been better if he had stayed on his own religion ... in matters of conscience there is a God on high Who judges, Who should be the consideration of the consciences of men, rather than kingdoms and crowns ... I expect only bad luck from it". (91).'

By the Edict of Nantes (1598), Henry IV gave the Huguenots religious freedom. But it was taken away again by Louis XIV in 1665: '*Article 3* We ordain that the Catholic, Apostolic and Roman faith be restored and re-established in all those districts and places of this our Realm ... in which its exercise has been interrupted, there to be freely and peaceably exercised. ...

Article 6 And to leave no occasion for trouble or difference among our subjects: We permit those of the so-called Reformed Religion to live and abide in all the towns and districts of this our Realm ...

free from inquisition, molestation or compulsion to do anything in the way of Religion, against their conscience ... provided that they observe the provisions of this Edict. ...

Article 9 We also permit those of the aforesaid Religion to practise it in all the towns and districts of our dominion, in which it had been established and publicly observed by them on several distinct occasions during the year 1596 and the year 1597 up to the end of August, all decrees and judgements to the contrary not-withstanding (92).'

Coins of Louis XIV commemorating the Revocation of the Edict of Nantes

Here is an extract from the speech made by Henry to the *Parlement* of Paris in 1599, which persuaded them to verify the Edict of Nantes: 'What I have to say is that I want you to verify the Edict which I have granted to those of the Religion. I have done it to bring about peace. I have made it abroad; I want it at home. You should obey me, even if there were no other consideration but my station and the obligation of subjects, but you, of my Parlement, have a special obligation. I restored their houses to some who had been exiled, their faith to others who had lost it. If obedience was due to my predecessors, it is due still more to me, as I have reestablished the state, God having chosen me to come into this heritage. The members of my Parlement would not be in office without me ... I know the road to sedition which led to the Barricades and the assassination of the late King. I'll take care it doesn't happen again ... (93).'

An Englishman spoke of the violent outbreak of image-breaking in Antwerp in 1566, following the spread of Calvinism there, and elsewhere in the Netherlands: 'I, with above ten thousand more, went into the churches to see what stir there was there; and coming into our Lady Church, it looked like a hell: where above 1000 torches burning, and such a noise! as if Heaven and Earth had gone down together, with falling of Images and beating down of costly works; in such sort that the spoil was so great that a man could not well pass through the church. So that, in fine, I cannot write you in ten sheets of paper the strange sight I saw there—organs and all, destroyed! and from thence I went (as the rest of the people did), to all the houses of Religion, where was the like stir—breaking and spoiling of all there was. Yet, they that this did, never looked towards any spoil, but broke all in pieces, and let it lie underfoot (94).'

A strong letter written by Philip to his Regent in the Netherlands in 1565 expresses his determination to crush Calvinism there: 'As to the Inquisition,' he wrote, 'my will is that it be enforced by the Inquisitors, as of old and as is required by all law, human and divine. This lies very near my heart and I require you to carry out my orders. Let all prisoners be put to death, and suffer them no longer to escape through the neglect, weakness and bad faith of the judges.' He added: 'If any are too timid to execute the edicts, I will replace them by men who have more heart and zeal (95).'

Philip declared he would destroy all heresy in the Netherlands; William of Orange, the most powerful nobleman in the country, was deeply upset: 'I confess I was deeply moved with pity for all the worthy people who were thus devoted to slaughter, and for the country to which I owed so much, wherein they designed to introduce an Inquisition worse and more cruel than that of Spain. I saw, as it were, nets spread to entrap the lords of the land as well as the people, so that those whom the Spaniards and their creatures could not supplant in any other way, might by this device fall into their hands. It was enough for a man to look askance at an image to be condemned to the stake. Seeing all this, I confess that from that hour I resolved with my whole soul to do my best to drive the Spanish vermin from the land; and of this resolve I have never repented, but believe that I, my comrades and all who have stood with us, have done a worthy deed, fit to be held in perpetual honour (96).'

In 1580 Philip angrily declared William an outlaw: 'Now we hereby declare this head and chief author of all the troubles to be a traitor and miscreant, an enemy of ourselves and our country. We interdict all our subjects from holding converse with him, from supplying him with lodging, food, water, or fire under pain of our royal indignation. And in execution of this Declaration we empower all and every to seize the person and the goods of this William of Nassau, as enemy of the human race; and hereby, on the word of

Philip II of Spain

a King and as minister of God, we promise to any one who has the heart to free us of this pest, and who will deliver him dead or alive, or take his life, the sum of 25,000 crowns in gold or in estates for himself and his heirs; we will pardon him any crime if he has been guilty, and give him a patent of nobility, if he be not noble, and we will do the same for all accomplices and agents. And we shall hold all who shall disobey this order as rebels, and will visit them with pains and penalties. And, lastly, we give command to all our governors to have this Declaration published in all parts of our said Provinces (97).'

William's defiance

William, however, defied Philip in an *Apology*, an open letter addressed to all the people of the Netherlands: 'I take it as a signal honour that I am the mark of the cruel and barbarous proscription hurled at me by the Spaniard for undertaking your cause and that of freedom and independence; and for this I am called traitor, heretic, foreigner, rebel, enemy of the human race, and I am to be killed like a wild beast, with a price offered to my assassins. I am no foreigner here, no rebel, no traitor (98).'

He went on, 'I was bred up a Catholic and a worldling, but the horrible persecution that I witnessed by fire, sword and water, and the plot to introduce a worse than Spanish Inquisition which I learned from the King of France, made me resolve in my soul to rest not till I have chased from the land these locusts of Spain ... And of the resistance to the tyranny of Spain I take responsibility, for I view with indignation the bloodthirsty cruelties, worse than those of any tyrant of antiquity, which they have inflicted upon the poor people of this land (99).'

Assassination of William

After several attempts on his life, William was brutally murdered in 1584. But a state document said of him: 'As long as he lived he was the guiding star of a whole brave nation, and when he died the little children cried in the streets (100).'

Passions ran high on every side. The stability and security of the medieval world was fast vanishing, and Europe stood on the brink of a new age. Much violence and bloodshed was to follow as old, cherished institutions were threatened. What was the church of Rome to do?

6 The Counter-Reformation

THE Counter-Reformation tried partly to reform the Roman Church from within, and partly to fight the spread of Protestantism. It began with the formation of new religious orders, the most important being the Society of Jesus founded in 1540 by Ignatius Loyola (1491–1556), a Spaniard. It became a powerful teaching and missionary society; the first and most famous of its missionaries was Francis Xavier, who worked from 1541 to 1552 in the East. The Council of Trent stated once and for all where Roman Catholicism differed from Protestantism, and drew up an important 'Profession of Faith' for everyone to follow. The Roman and Spanish Inquisitions were developed to destroy heresy; and the Papacy was reformed and modernised to give the Church a new dynamic leadership.

Lainez, one of Loyola's original companions, spoke of his qualities of leadership: 'Great knowledge of the things of God, and great devotion to them, and the more metaphysical these matters were, and over our heads, the better he knew them; great good sense and prudence in matters of business; the divine gift of discretion; great fortitude and magnanimity in tribulation; great guilelessness in not judging others and in putting a favourable interpretation on all things; and great skill in knowing how to set himself and others to work for the service of God (101).' *Ignatius Loyola*

Another follower, Ribadeneira, was impressed by Loyola's calmness: 'Often and often we have seen him, in perfect calmness and with all the sweetness of manner that can be imagined, order someone brought before him for punishment; and when the offender came into his presence, it seemed as if he was transformed and all afire; and then, after he had finished speaking and the offender had gone, immediately, without the slightest interval of time he returned to his former serenity and blitheness of countenance, as if nothing had happened. It was clear that there had been no irritation whatever within, and that he had made use of that sudden look as a mask, putting it on and laying it aside at will ... (102).'

Ribadeneira attributed this calmness to Loyola's saintly self-control: 'And though his bodily condition had its ups and downs, for his health was inconstant, nevertheless his soul was invariably of an even temper. What I mean is that if you wished to ask for something from Father Ignatius, it made no difference whether he was on his way from mass or had had dinner, or whether he had just got out of bed, or had been at prayer, whether he had received good news or bad, whether things were quiet, or the world upside down. With him there was no such thing as "feeling his pulse", no "taking a reckoning by the North Star, no steering by a sea chart", as is the usual way of dealing with men in authority, for he was always in a state of calm self-mastery (103).'

From the diary of one who knew Loyola, we know that Loyola was very frugal: 'His table was always resplendent with parsimony and frugality, but it had nevertheless a savour of gentle usages. There were two or three brothers to wait upon it, more especially when outsiders were invited to dinner. The wine glasses were served with elegance; it could not have been better done, or more attractively, in a palace (104).'

Ribadeneira has another recollection: 'I have often seen him, in his old age, standing out on the balcony, or on some place of vantage where he could look at the sky, fix his gaze upwards and remain motionless, lost in thought, for a long time, and then, overcome by emotion, shed tears of joy. And I have often heard him say: "How contemptible the world seems when I look up at the sky" (105).'

Obedient men Ribadeneira told a story which showed how Loyola insisted upon total obedience among his followers, an obedience which was to make the Jesuits both admired and feared: 'Father Ignatius and I were strolling about together after supper, and a good many others were walking about and talking of one thing or another at a little distance off. While we two were discussing spiritual matters, Father

Ignatius paused, and stepping up to one of the brothers said: "Go, see who those are walking over yonder". The brother came back and said it was one of our priests talking to a novice. Ignatius called the priest up and asked, "What were you talking about to the novice?" The priest replied: "Father, we got on the topic of humility and mortification, and I was telling him what I had seen myself, or had heard, in those respects, about Brother Texeda [who was not a member of the Society of Jesus] in order to encourage the lad to follow his pattern". Father Ignatius said: "Are there no examples to be found in the Society, that you go seeking them from outsiders? Who gave you permission to talk to novices, when you have not sense enough? Go to the minister and bid him strike your name off that list, and don't speak again to a novice without leave from me" (106).'

Ignatius Loyola

In the Constitution (rules) of the Society of Jesus, Loyola set out what obedience should mean: 'And let each one persuade himself that they that live under obedience ought to allow themselves to be borne and ruled by divine providence working through their Superiors exactly as if they were a corpse which suffers itself to be borne and handled in any way whatsoever; or just as an old man's stick which serves him who holds it in his hand wherever and for whatever purpose he wish to use it ... (107).'

Rules for the Jesuits

The first of the *Rules for Thinking with the Church* in the *Spiritual Exercises* drawn up by Loyola for the Jesuits, reads: 'Always to be ready to obey with mind and heart, setting aside all judgement of one's own, the true spouse of Jesus Christ, our holy mother, our infallible and orthodox mistress, the Catholic Church, whose authority is exercised over us by the hierarchy (108).'

Jesuits were also told to encourage devotion to the Church among Roman Catholics: 'To commend to the faithful frequent and devout assistance at the holy sacrifice of the Mass, the ecclesiastical hymns, the divine office, and in general the prayers and devotions practised at stated times, whether in public in the churches or in private (109).'

Francis Xavier's voyage

An account is given by the surgeon of the ship on which Francis Xavier, the great Jesuit missionary, sailed to the East. It is a vivid picture of a great saint: 'I came out from Portugal on the same ship as Father Francis and I often watched him at his charitable occupations and whilst he taught Christian doctrine. He used to beg alms from other passengers for the poor and sick persons. He took personal charge of such as were ailing or prostrated by illness. From this work of mercy, and from his hearing of confessions, he allowed himself never a moment's respite, but cheerfully accomplished it all. Everybody held him for a saint, and that was my own fixed opinion. At Mozambique the Father gave himself so completely to the service of those who were taken from the five ships who were already ill, and to those who fell ill afterwards during the winter spent on the island, that only forty or forty-one of the sufferers died. Everybody regarded this as a marvellous thing, indeed as a real miracle due under God to the devotedness and goodness of the Father. He fell sick himself in consequence of his crushing labours, and I took him to my lodging to take care of him. So bad did he become that I had to bleed him nine times, and for three whole days he was out of his senses. I noticed that while in delirium he raved unintelligibly about other things, but in speaking of the things of God was perfectly lucid and coherent. As soon as he was convalescent, he resumed his former labours with all his old enthusiasm (110).'

A fellow-Jesuit who saw Xavier at work in India shows how well

Xavier worked among ordinary people: 'He went up and down the streets and squares with a bell in his hand, crying to the children and others to come to the instructions. The novelty of the proceeding, never seen before in Goa, brought a large crowd around him which he then led to the church. He began by singing the lessons which he had rhymed and then made the children sing them so that they might become the better fixed in their memories. Afterwards he explained each point in the simplest way, using only such words as his young audience could readily understand. By this method, which has since been adopted everywhere in the Indies, he so deeply engrained the truths and precepts of the faith in the hearts of the people that men and women, children and old folk, took to singing the ten commandments while they walked in the streets, as did the fisherman in his boat and the labourer in the fields, for their own entertainment and recreation (111).' *Xavier in India*

The Council of Trent (1545–63) was set up to try to sort out the religious confusion now felt by many people. As its starting point, it gave equal authority to Scripture and Tradition: 'Following the example of the orthodox Fathers, this synod receives and venerates, with equal pious affection and reverence, all the books both of the New and the Old Testaments, since one God is the author of both, together with the said Traditions, as well those pertaining to faith as those pertaining to morals, as having been given either from the lips of Christ, or by the dictation of the Holy Spirit and preserved by unbroken succession in the Catholic Church ... (112).' *Council of Trent: Scripture and tradition*

The Council also refused to ban the practice of indulgences. The reason was: 'Since the power of conferring indulgences has been granted to the Church by Christ, and since the Church has made use of this divinely given power even from the earliest times, the holy Synod teaches and enjoins that the use of indulgences, which is greatly salutary for Christian people and has been approved by the authority of sacred Councils, is to be retained in the Church ... (113).'

Finally, it supported the age-old veneration of images in churches: 'And the bishops shall carefully teach this: that, by means of the stories of the mysteries of our Redemption, portrayed by paintings and other representations, the people are instructed and confirmed in the habit of remembering, and continually revolving in mind the *Use of images*

articles of faith; as also that great profit is derived from all sacred images, not only because the people are thereby admonished of the benefits and gifts bestowed upon them by Christ, but also because the miracles which God has performed by means of the Saints and their salutary examples are set before the eyes of the faithful; that they may give God thanks for those things, may order their own lives and manners in imitation of the Saints; and may be excited to adore and love God and to cultivate piety (114).'

From 1564, the clergy had to make a public statement of their beliefs, to avoid confusion. Here is an extract from this statement, known as 'the Tridentine Profession of Faith': 'I recognize the Holy Catholic and Apostolic Roman Church as the mother and mistress of all churches; and I vow and swear true obedience to the Roman Pontiff, the successor of blessed Peter, the chief of the Apostles and the representative [*vicarius*] of Jesus Christ (115).' *Tridentine Profession of Faith (1564)*

But all these measures did not stop the growth of Protestantism. A Swiss traveller wrote in 1599 of how an obstinate Protestant would be treated by the Spanish Inquisition: 'If he refuses to be converted, he is sent to a large town to be burned on the pyre, perhaps alone, perhaps with others like him. Wearing a gown on which are pictures of devils pulling him into hell and tormenting him in a thousand ways, he is thus put to death in the most atrocious manner, and his picture is exhibited in the cathedrals to perpetuate his shame; but for the martyrs this death is glory, as indeed it is thus to suffer persecution and death for the true religion of Jesus Christ (116).' *Inquisition in Spain*

At the same time, the papacy did do much to modernise itself. The Conclaves, for example, at which the Cardinals elected a new Pope, had been filled with intrigue and scandal, but as a Cardinal wrote in 1579, Pope Gregory XIII had improved matters: 'I can say with truth that I have never seen, in any of the Conclaves at which I have been present, any Cardinal or member lose control of himself; I have indeed seen very few of them grow warm. It is rare to hear a raised voice or to see an angry face. I have often tried to find some difference in the look of those who had just been defeated, and I can say with truth that, with one single exception, I have never found any. So remote is even the suspicion of those revenges with which Italy is usually wrongly charged, that it is even common *Papal reform*

67

Facing page A French bookseller is burned at the stake at Avignon for selling Bibles in the French language

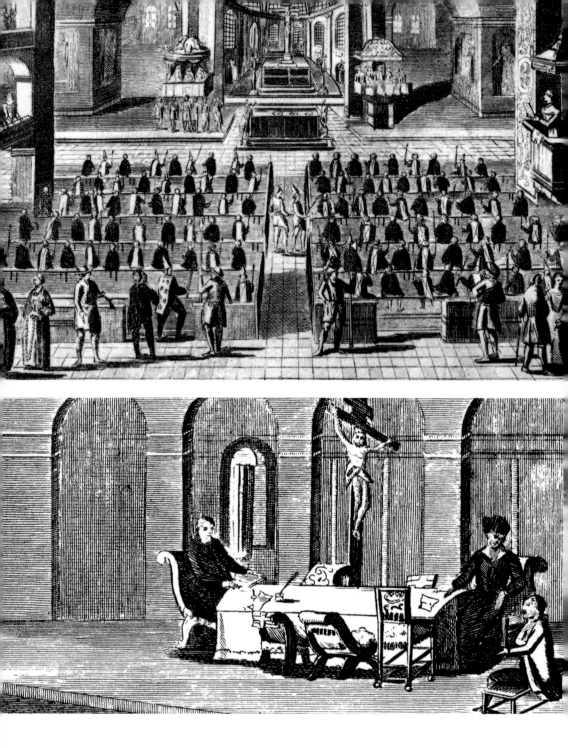

Above The *auto-da-fée* celebrated during the Spanish Inquisition, and *below* examining those who refused to make the act of faith

Above Burning those condemned in the Spanish Inquisition. *Below left* the dress of a man condemned to death, and *below right* the dress of a penitent reprieved from death

enough for an opponent to drink at dinner the wine which the candidate whom he has defeated that morning has just sent him. In a word, I dare say that there is nothing more wise or grand than the ordinary scene in a Conclave. I know well that the procedure practised there since the Bull of Gregory contributes greatly to regulate it; but it must be admitted that only Italians are capable of observing this order with as much decorum as is necessary (117).

7 England: The Beginnings of Protestantism

IN ENGLAND John Wycliffe (1325–84) had spoken out against several aspects of the Medieval Church, and the Lollards, his followers, were persecuted until the sixteenth century. Everyone knew that the clergy were below standard, and monasteries had a reputation for wealth and good living rather than Christian example. Several had already been dissolved. The new books of Erasmus and Luther gained support in England, and so did the efforts of William Tyndale to produce a Bible which everyone could read (ordinary people could not read the old Latin Bibles). Popular opinion was hostile to the clergy and ready to help bring the Church out of the Middle Ages into modern times.

The Lollards strongly objected to the Church being so rich, as *Lollard beliefs* we learn from their statement to Parliament in 1394: 'That when the Church of England began to go mad after temporalities, like its great step-mother the Roman Church, and churches were authorized by appropriation in divers places, faith, hope, and charity began to flee from our Church, because pride, with its doleful progeny of mortal sins, claimed this under title of truth. This conclusion is general, and proved by experience, custom, and manner or fashion (118).'

They were also worried about the Mass: 'That the pretended miracle of the sacrament of bread drives all men, but a few, to idolatry, because they think that the Body of Christ which is never away from heaven could by power of the priest's word be enclosed essentially in a little bread which they show the people (119).'

In the same year the King issued Letters Patent condemning the *Lollards* Lollards and giving the Archbishops of Canterbury and York power *condemned* to punish them: 'Being moved by zeal for the Catholic faith, of which we are and wish to be defenders in all things as we are bound, being unwilling in any wise to tolerate such heresies or errors springing up, have within the limit of our power granted authority and licence by our letters patent to the archbishop aforesaid and his suffragans, to arrest all and singular those who should wish secretly or openly to preach or maintain the aforesaid conclusions so condemned, wherever they may be found, and commit them, at pleasure, to their own prisons or [to the prisons] of others, to be kept in the same until they repent of the wickedness of their errors and heresies (120).'

A Wycliffite martyr Many Lollards were burned at the stake. Here is an unsympathetic account of the burning of a Lollard in 1494: 'Upon the eighteenth day of April was an old cankered heretic, weak-minded for age, named Joan Boughton, widow, and mother unto the wife of Sir John Young—which daughter, as some reported, had a great smell of an heretic after the mother—burnt in Smithfield. This woman was four score years of age or more, and held eight opinions of heresy which I pass over, for the hearing of them is neither pleasant nor fruitful. She was a disciple of Wyclif, whom she accounted for a saint, and held so fast and firmly eight of his twelve opinons that all the doctors of London could not turn her from one of them. When it was told to her that she should be burnt for her obstinacy and false belief, she set nought at their words but defied them, for she said she was so beloved with God and His holy angels that all the fire in London should not hurt her. But on the morrow a bundle of faggots and a few reeds consumed her in a little while; and while she might cry she spake often of God and Our Lady, but no man could cause her to name Jesus, and so she died. But it appeared that she left some of her disciples behind her, for the night following, the more part of the ashes of that fire that she was burnt in were had away and kept for a precious relic in an earthen pot (121).'

Persecution of Lollards John Foxe wrote in his *Acts and Monuments* that these persecutions brought disgrace to Christian people: 'In turning over the registers and records of Lincoln likewise, and coming to the year of our Lord 1520, and to 1521, I find that as the light of the Gospel began more to appear, and the number of [its] professors to grow, so the vehemency of persecution and stir of the bishops began also

Facing page Lollards imprisoned in the Tower of London

George King

John Wade

T. Leye

Andrew

to increase; whereupon ensued great perturbation and grievous affliction in divers and sundry quarters of this realm, especially about Buckinghamshire and Amersham, Uxbridge, Henley, Newbury, in the diocese of London, in Essex, Colchester, Suffolk and Norfolk, and other parts more. And this was before the name of Luther was heard of in these countries among the people. Wherefore they are much beguiled and misinformed, who condemn this kind of doctrine now received, of novelty; asking, "Where was this church and religion forty years ago, before Luther's time". To whom it may be answered, that this religion and form of doctrine was planted by the Apostles, and taught by true bishops; afterward decayed, and now reformed again ... (122).'

Foxe listed the four main Lollard beliefs: 'Four principal points they stood in against the Church of Rome: in pilgrimage, in adoration of saints, in reading Scripture-books in English, and in the carnal presence of Christ's body in the sacrament (123).'

A sermon preached at an ordination service in 1510 by Dr William Melton, Chancellor of York Minster, stressed the need for better education and morals among the parish clergy: 'For it is from this stupidity and from this darkness of ignorance that there arises that great and deplorable evil throughout the whole Church of God, that everywhere throughout town and countryside there exists a crop of oafish and boorish priests, some of whom are engaged on ignoble and servile tasks, while others abandon themselves to tavern-haunting, swilling and drunkenness. Some cannot get along without their wenches; others pursue their amusement in dice and gambling and other such trifling all day long. There are some who waste their time in hunting and hawking, and so spend a life which is utterly and wholly slothful and irreligious even to advanced old age. This is inevitable, for since they are all completely ignorant of good literature, how can they obtain improvement or enjoyment in reading and study? Nay rather, they throw aside their books in contempt and everywhere they return to the wretched and unlovely life I have mentioned, and seek to satisfy their sloth and idleness in trifles of this sort ... (124).'

Need for reform

Conditions in a monastery were reported after a visitation (inspection) of Ramsey Abbey by the Bishop of Lincoln in 1518: 'The gates of the monastery are not shut securely at night for the

Conditions in a monastery

75

lord abbot nor are the walls and closes of the monastery sufficient. The monks of the monastery can get out of the monastery at will in the night. And also outsiders and seculars enter the monastery at night time, also the conventual church, so that recently there was furtively taken from the conventual church at night, a chalice, in what way or by whom is not known. The bishop charged the abbot and prior that the walls and enclosures of the monastery should be adequate by the feast of All Souls, and that the gates should be sufficiently shut so that no monks should in any way be able to leave nor outsiders to enter (125).'

Precedent for dissolution A licence issued in 1509 allowed St John's Priory, Cambridge, to be converted into St John's College: 'Executors of Margaret, Countess of Richmond. Licence to Richard Fox, bishop of Winchester, John Fisher, bishop of Rochester, Charles Somerset, Lord Herbert, Sir Thomas Lovell, Sir Henry Marney, Sir John Seynt John, Harry Hornby, clerk, and Hugh Assheton clerk, executors of the Countess; to acquire the site and possessions of the priory of St John the Evangelist, Cambridge, in the patronage of James, bishop of Ely, by right of his church, and now in a most impoverished and delapidated condition, and convert the same into a college for a master, fellows, and scholars (in pursuance of the wish of the said Countess), to be called The College of St John the Evangelist, Cambridge (126).'

Thomas Bilney's conversion In the early 1500s, many people were converted to Protestantism. An early Protestant, Thomas Bilney of Cambridge, tells of his conversion in 1516 after buying a copy of Erasmus's Latin version of the New Testament: 'I bought it even by the providence of God, as I do now well understand and perceive: and at the first reading (as I well remember) I chanced upon this sentence of St Paul (O most sweet and comfortable sentence to my soul!) in *I Timothy*, i: "It is a true saying, and worthy of all men to be embraced, that Christ Jesus came into the world to save sinners, of whom I am the chief and principal." This one sentence, through God's instruction and inward working, which I did not then perceive, did so exhilarate my heart, being before wounded with the guilt of my sins, and being almost in despair, that immediately I felt a marvellous comfort and quietness (127).'

76 Bilney in turn converted Robert Barnes, the Prior of the August-

Facing page Thomas Bilney burned at the stake for his beliefs

inian Friary in Cambridge: 'The first sermon that ever he preached of this truth was the Sunday before Christmas day [1525] at St Edward's church, belonging to Trinity Hall in Cambridge by the Peas-market, whose theme was the Epistle of the same Sunday, *Gaudete in Domino*, etc.; and so postilled [commented upon] the whole Epistle, following the Scripture and Luther's Postil; and for that sermon he was immediately accused of heresy by two fellows of the King's Hall. Then the godly learned in Christ both of Pembroke Hall, St John's, Peterhouse, Queen's College, the King's College, Gonville Hall and Benet College showed themselves and flocked together in open sight, both in the schools and at open sermons at St Mary's and at the Augustines and at other disputations; and then they conferred continually together (128).'

Bilney, Barnes and other Cambridge scholars met secretly to discuss Luther's books in the White Horse Inn during the 1520s: 'The house that they resorted most commonly unto was the White Horse which for despite of them, to bring God's word into contempt, was called Germany. This house especially was chosen because many of them of St John's, the King's College and the Queen's College, came in on the back side (129).'

A visiting teacher from London who had recently been in Germany read and talked to a group of Buckinghamshire Lollards at their usual meeting for Scripture-reading; this account was taken from their trial in 1530: 'These persons with others were examined, excommunicated, and abjured, for being together in John Taylor's house at Hughenden, and there hearing Nicholas Field of London read a parcel of Scripture in English unto them, who were expounded to them many things; as that they that went on pilgrimage were accursed: that it booted not to pray to images, for they were but stocks made of wood, and could not help a man: that God Almighty biddeth us work as well one day as another, saving the Sunday; for six days he wrought, and the seventh day he rested: that they needed not to fast so many fasting days, except the ember days; for he [Field] was beyond the sea in Almany [Germany], and there they used not so to fast, nor to make such holy days (130).'

Tyndale had long wanted to translate the New Testament into English. His translation was at last printed in 1525. Here, he argues the need for a Bible which ordinary people could understand: 'Christ commandeth to search the scriptures. John v. Though that miracles bore record unto his doctrine, yet desired he no faith to be given either to his doctrine, or to his miracles, without record of the scripture. When Paul preached, Acts xvii the other searched the scriptures daily, whether they were as he alleged them. Why shall not I likewise see whether it be the scripture that thou allegest? Yea, why shall I not see the scripture, and the circumstances, and what goeth before and after; that I may know whether thine interpretation be the right sense, or whether thou jugglest, and drawest the scripture violently unto thy carnal and fleshly purpose; or whether thou be about to teach me, or to deceive me? (131).'

William Tyndale who translated the New Testament into English

A confession made in 1527 by an Essex Lollard tells how Robert Barnes, at the Austin Friary in London, secretly sold them a copy of Tyndale's New Testament, to replace their old Latin hand-written Gospels: 'Thomas Hilles and this respondent showed the Friar Barnes of certain old books that they had; as of four Evangel-

Tyndale's Bible obtained by Essex Lollards

79

ists, and certain Epistles of Peter and Paul in English, which books the said Friar did little regard, and made a twit of it, and said, "A point for them, for they be not to be regarded toward [compared with] the new printed Testament in English, for it is of more cleaner English". And then the said Friar Barnes delivered to them the said New Testament in English, for which they paid 3s. 2d., and desired them that they would keep it close (132).'

The Bishop of London tricked (1529)
Tyndale's New Testaments had to be printed on the Continent and secretly smuggled into London by friendly English merchants. One of these, Augustine Packington, was asked by Cuthbert Tunstall, Bishop of London, to buy copies so that he might throw them on a blazing fire as an example to the people of England: 'Augustine Packington came to William Tyndale and said, "William, I know thou art a poor man, and hast a heap of New Testaments and books by thee, for the which thou hast endangered thy friends and beggared thyself, and I have now gotten thee a merchant, which with ready money shall dispatch thee of all that thou hast, if you think it so profitable for yourself." "Who is the merchant?" said Tyndale. "The Bishop of London", said Packington. "O, that is because he will burn them," said Tyndale. "Yea, Mary", quod Packington. "I am the gladder", said Tyndale, "for these two benefits shall come thereof; I shall get money of him for these books, to bring myself out of debt, and the whole world shall cry out upon the burning of God's word. And the overplus of the money that shall remain to me shall make me more studious to correct the said New Testament, and so newly to imprint the same once again, and I trust the second will much better like you than ever did the first." (133).'

Grievances against the clergy
An extract from *A Supplication for the Beggars* written by Simon Fish about 1529 expresses a common dislike of the clergy: 'These are not the [shep]herds but the ravenous wolves going in [shep]herds' clothing, devouring the flock: the bishops, abbots, priors, deacons, archdeacons, suffragans, priests, monks, canons, friars, pardoners and summoners. And who is able to number this idle, ravenous sort, which (setting all labour aside) have begged so importunately that they have gotten into their hands more than the third part of all your realm. The goodliest lordships, manors, lands and territories are theirs (134).'

This, then, was the background of religious feeling in England, which closely paralled developments on the Continent. Yet the English Reformation developed along a road of its own, and was given special impetus by Henry VIII's domestic problems—in particular, his need for a quick divorce from Catherine of Aragon.

King Henry the eyght.

8 England: The Henrician Reformation

THE REFORMATION under Henry VIII (1509–47) was largely political, unlike the Reformation on the Continent, and was sparked off by his divorce problems. Papal authority over the Church of England was taken by the Crown, the monasteries were dissolved and the monks turned out. An English Bible was officially printed for people to read in the churches. But Henry was basically conservative in his religious outlook and did not really wish to help the Protestants too far. Like other Heads of State, his main interest was national unity.

A French writer who visited the Vatican Library in 1581, saw *'Defender of* the book which Henry VIII wrote against Luther's teaching. Henry *the Faith'* sent copies to the Pope, and in return the Pope gratefully gave him the title of 'Defender of the Faith': 'The original of the book that the King of England composed against Luther, which he sent about fifty years ago to Pope Leo X, inscribed with his own hand: "To Leo Ten, Henry, King of the English, sends This work, a pledge of loyalty between two friends." I read the prefaces, the one to the Pope, the other to the reader: he excuses himself because of his military occupations and lack of ability; for scholastic Latin it is good (135).'

In 1527 Henry VIII asked the Pope to dissolve his marriage with *The Sack of* Catherine of Aragon. But the Pope had other things to worry about. *Rome (1527)* The troops of Emperor Charles V, Catherine's nephew, had just sacked and occupied Rome. Here is an eyewitness account of the sack of Rome: 'The soldiers slew at pleasure; pillaged the houses of the middle classes and small folk, the palaces of the nobles, the convents of both sexes, and the churches. They made prisoners

83

Facing page Henry VIII attending Parliament

of men, women, and even of little children, without regard to age, or vows, or any other claim on pity. The slaughter was not great, for men rarely kill those who offer no resistance; but the booty was incalculable, in coin, jewels, gold and silver plate, clothes, tapestries, furniture, and goods of all descriptions. To this should be added the ransoms, which amounted to a sum which, if set down, would win no credence (136).'

The Reformation Parliament (1529)

But Henry VIII was in a hurry for his divorce from Catherine of Aragon. As the Pope had not helped him, he summoned a Parliament in 1529 which was to carry out the Reformation. Parliament at once began to complain about the Church: 'The sixth cause was to see one priest being little learned to have ten or twelve benefices and to be resident on none, and to know many well-learned scholars in the university, which were able to preach and teach, to have neither benefice nor exhibition (137).'

A list of charges against the ordinaries (i.e. bishops) was drawn up by the House of Commons and sent to the King. Among the charges it made was: 'And also the said spiritual ordinaries do daily confer and give sundry benefices unto certain young folks, calling them their nephews or kinsfolk, being in their minority ... apt ne able to serve the cure of any such benefice; whereby the said ordinaries do keep and detain the fruits and profits of the same benefices in their own hands ... and the poor silly [simple] souls of your people and subjects ... for lack of good curates do perish without good example, doctrine or any good teaching (138).'

Submission of the Clergy (1532)

Henry was pleased. He made the clergy promise that they would never again make any church law without royal permission: 'First, do offer and promise, *in verbo sacerdotii*, here unto your Highness, submitting ourselves most humbly to the same, that we will never from henceforth enact ... or execute any new canons or constitutions provincial, or any other new ordinance, provincial or synodal, in our Convocation or Synod in time coming, which Convocation is, alway hath been, and must be, assembled only by your Highness's commandment of writ, unless your Highness by your royal assent shall licence us to assemble our Convocation, and to ... execute such constitutions ... and thereto give your royal assent and authority (139).'

Henry moved fast. In the same year (1532), Parliament passed an

Act stopping the payment of 'annates' to the Pope by the clergy. *First Act of*
Its operation was delayed until the Pope approved the consecration *Annates*
of Thomas Cranmer as new Archbishop of Canterbury; but this he *(1532)*
did early in 1533: 'It is therefore ordained, established, and enacted,
by authority of this present Parliament, that the unlawful payments
of annates, or first fruits, and all manner contributions for the same,
for any archbishopric or bishopric, or for any bulls hereafter to be
obtained from the Court of Rome, to or for the aforesaid purpose
and intent, shall from henceforth utterly cease, and no such hereafter to be paid for any archbishopric or bishopric within this realm
(140).'

Henry's plans for divorce were now nearing completion. In 1533, *Act in*
he made Parliament pass an 'Act in Restraint of Appeals'. This was *Restraint of*
to prevent Catherine of Aragon appealing to the Pope against her *Appeals*
divorce which was to be determined by Cranmer: '[such] causes ... *(1533)*
shall be from henceforth heard, examined, discussed, clearly,
finally, and definitively adjudged and determined within the King's
jurisdiction and authority, and not elsewhere, in such courts spiritual
and temporal of the same, as the natures, conditions, and qualities
of the causes ... shall require ... any foreign inhibitions, appeals,
sentences ... interdictions, excommunications, restraints, judgments,
or any other process ... from the see of Rome, or any other foreign
courts or potentates of the world ... notwithstanding (141).'

When this was done, Cranmer pronounced the divorce: 'We *Catherine*
Thomas Archbishop, primate, and legate aforesaid, having first in- *divorced*
voked the name of Christ and with God alone before our eyes, pro- *(1533)*
nounce decree and declare the nullity and invalidity of the said
marriage, and that this same pretended marriage was and is null and
void, and was contracted and consummated contrary to divine love,
and is of no value or consequence but was lacking and lacks force
and legal confirmation, and that the aforesaid most illustrious and
most mighty prince Henry VIII, and the most high lady Catherine
ought not to remain in the same pretended matrimony (142).'

A Second Act of Annates (1534) not only withheld annates for *Second Act*
all time, but also handed over the appointment of bishops to the *of Annates*
Crown: 'At every avoidance [vacancy] of every archbishopric or *(1534)*
bishopric within this realm, or in any other the King's dominions,
the King our Sovereign Lord, his heirs and successors, may grant

unto the prior and convent, or the dean and chapter of the cathedral churches or monasteries where the see of such archbishopric or bishopric shall happen to be void, a licence under the great seal, as of old time hath been accustomed, to proceed to election of an archbishop or bishop of the see so being void, with a letter missive, containing the name of the person which they shall elect and choose: by virtue of which licence the said dean and chapter, or prior and convent, to whom any such licence and letters missives shall be directed, shall with all speed and celerity in due form elect and choose the said person named in the said letters missives, to the dignity and office of the archbishopric or bishopric so being void, and none other (143).'

A further act now made the clergy pay annates to the Crown instead of to the Pope: 'It may therefore be ordained and enacted ... that the King's Highness, his heirs and successors ... shall have and enjoy from time to time, to endure for ever, of every such person ... which at any time after the first day of January next coming shall be nominated, elected ... presented, collated, or by any other means appointed to have any archbishopric, bishopric, abbacy, monastery, priory, college, hospital, archdeaconry, deanery, provostship, prebend, parsonage, vicarage, chantry, free chapel, or other dignity, benefice, office or promotion spiritual within this realm or elsewhere within any of the King's dominions, of what name, nature or quality soever they be or to whose foundation, patronage or gift soever they belong, the first fruits, revenues and profits for one year of every such archbishopric, bishopric [and all benefices and ecclesiastical offices mentioned above] ... and that every such person ... before any actual or real possession or meddling with the profits of any such archbishopric, bishopric [etc.] ... shall satisfy, content and pay, or compound or agree to pay to the King's use at reasonable days upon good sureties the said first fruits and profits for one year (144).'

Henry completed the Reformation by the Act of Supremacy (1534): 'Be it enacted by authority of this present Parliament, that the King our Sovereign Lord, his heirs and successors, kings of this realm, shall be taken, accepted, and reputed the only Supreme Head in earth of the Church of England, called *Anglicana Ecclesia*, and shall have and enjoy, annexed and united to the imperial Crown of

Act of Supremacy (1534)

Facing page Thomas Cranmer

Left Henry VIII and *right* Anne Boleyn

this realm, as well the title and style thereof, as all honours, dignities, pre-eminences, jurisdictions, privileges, authorities, immunities, profits, and commodities, to the said dignity of Supreme Head of the same Church belonging and appertaining (145).'

Everyone in the English Church had to acknowledge Henry VIII as Supreme Head on Earth of the Church of England. Here is the acknowledgement made by the Abbot and monks of Peterborough Abbey in 1534: 'We the said Abbot and Convent and our successors all and singular, will always display entire, inviolate, sincere and perpetual, fidelity, regard and obedience towards our Lord King Henry the eighth, and towards Queen Anne his wife, and towards his offspring of the same Anne legitimately as well begotten as to be begotten. And that we will notify, preach, and persuade these same things to the people wherever place and opportunity shall be given. Also that we always hold it confirmed and established, and always will hold, that the aforesaid Henry our King is the head of the Church of England. And also that the bishop of Rome, who in his

Sir Thomas More

bulls takes the name of Pope, and claims for himself the pre-eminence of chief pontiff, has no other greater jurisdiction assigned to him by God in this realm of England than any other foreign bishop (146).'

Sir Thomas More, however, was executed in 1535 for refusing to accept the Royal Supremacy. In his last speech, after being sentenced to death, he denied that he was taking a lone stand against the English bishops and universities who supported the Act: '"Neither as yet", said he, "have I chanced upon any ancient writer or doctor that so advanceth, as your Statute doth, the supremacy of any secular and temporal prince. If there were no more but myself upon my side, and the whole Parliament upon the other, I would be sore afraid to lean to mine own mind only against so many. But if the number of bishops and universities be so material as your lordship seemeth to take it, then see I little cause, my Lord, why that thing in my conscience should make any change. For I nothing doubt but that, though not in this realm, yet in Christendom about, of these well-

Sir Thomas More rebels

89

learned bishops and virtuous men that are still alive, they be not the fewer part that are of my mind therein. But if I should speak of those that are already dead, of whom many be now holy saints in heaven, I am very sure it is the far greater part of them that, all the while they lived, thought in this case that way that I think now; and therefore am I not bounden, my Lord, to conform my conscience to the Council of one realm against the general Council of Christendom. For of the foresaid holy bishops I have, for every bishop of yours, above one hundred. And for one Council or Parliament of yours (God knoweth what manner of one), I have all the Councils made these thousand years. And for this one Kingdom, I have all other Christian realms." (147).'

Sir Thomas More's house in Chelsea

More's wife, Mistress Alice, visited him in prison before his execution and could not understand why, for the sake of an oath, he had thrown away his life: '"Is not this house [prison]", quoth he, "as nigh heaven as my own?" To whom she, after her accustomed homely fashion, not liking such talk, answered "Tilly vally, Tilly vally." (148).'

In 1535 Thomas Cromwell, Henry's chief minister, sent out commissioners to inspect the monasteries. This is a report by one of
them on several in Oxfordshire: 'Pleaseth you to be advertised that
after my departing from Oxford I went to Godstow where I found
all things well and in good order as well in the monastery ..., as
also in the convent of the same, except that one sister 13 or 14 years
past, being then of another house, brake her chastity ... the which
for correction and punishment afterward was sent to Godstow
by the Bishop of Lincoln, where now and ever since that time she
hath lived virtuous.

'And from that house ... I came to a house of nuns called Catesby,
of £90 lands yearly, of the order of Citeaux, under my lord of
Lincoln's jurisdiction (as I suppose) by usurpation. For that order
as you know hath always been exempt from the Bishop. The prioress
there is a right sad matron, the sisters also there now being by the
space of 20 years hath been (by as much as I can learn) without
suspicion of incontinent living.

'From Catesby I rode to Canons Ashby, which house is £160 in
debt, by reason of the late preferment of the prior there now being.
The house also, by the negligence of his predecessor, is in ruin and
decay. Howbeit the said prior (although he be unlearned) is disposed
to thrive, and by the learning and good example of ... the sub-prior
... the religious men there be like to do well.

'From Canons Ashby, I rode to Chacombe; the prior is newly
come thither, who is competently well learned in holy Scripture.
The canons being rude and unlearned, he beginneth to bring them
to some order. I fear nothing in him but negligence and overmuch
familiarity, which he useth amongst them (149).'

Relics were seized by another commissioner from Maiden
Bradley Priory in Wiltshire, and sent to Cromwell as evidence of
monastic corruption: 'By this bringer my servant, I send you relics;
first, two flowers wrapped in white and black sarcenet that on
Christmas eve [in the hour on which Christ was born], will spring and
burgeon and bear blossoms [which may be put to the test], saith the
prior of Maiden Bradley: ye shall also receive a bag of relics, wherein ye shall see strange things, as shall appear by the Scripture, as,
God's coat, Our Lady's smock, part of God's supper ... [part of
the stone of the manger in which was born Jesus in Bethlehem];

belike there is in Bethlehem plenty of stones and some quarry, and maketh their mangers of stone (150).'

Small monasteries dissolved (1536)
After the commissioners had reported, Parliament passed an Act dissolving about 250 of the smaller monasteries: 'That it may be enacted by authority of this present Parliament, that his Majesty shall have and enjoy to him and to his heirs for ever, all and singular such monasteries, priories, and other religious houses of monks, canons, and nuns, of what kinds or diversities of habits, rules, or orders soever they be called or named, which have not in lands and tenements, rents, tithes, portions, and other hereditaments, above the clear yearly value of two hundred pounds (151).'

Pilgrimage of Grace (1536)
The dissolution of the monasteries produced a nothern rising, the Pilgrimage of Grace. This is an extract from the oath drawn up by the Yorkshire leader, Robert Aske, for the insurgents: 'Ye shall not enter into our said Pilgrimage for no particular profit to yourself, nor to do any displeasure to any private person, but by counsel of the commonwealth, nor slay nor murder for no envy, but in your hearts put away fear and dread and take afore you the Cross of Christ, and in your hearts His faith, the Restitution of the Church, the suppression of these Heretics and their opinions (152).'

The first verse of this ballad, thought to have been composed by the monks of Sawley Abbey in Lancashire, referred to the Pilgrimage of Grace:

> *'Crist crucifyd!*
> *For they woundes wide*
> *Us commens guyde!*
> *Which pilgrames be,*
> *Thrughe godes grace,*
> *For to purchache*
> *Olde welth and peax*
> *Of the spiritualtie (153).'*

Aske defends the monasteries
But the Pilgrimage failed. Henry would not listen. Aske was arrested, and thrown into the Tower of London. When he was questioned, he spoke up for the monasteries: 'Also the abbeys was one of the beauties of this realm to all men and strangers passing through the same; also all gentlemen much succoured in their needs with money, their young sons there succoured, and in nunneries their daughters brought up in virtue; ... and such abbeys as were

92

near the danger of sea banks [were] great maintainers of sea walls and dykes, maintainers and builders of bridges and highways [and] such other things for the common wealth (154).'

Between 1537 and 1539 many larger monasteries were persuaded to surrender to the King. This deed of surrender of the Cistercian Abbey of Furness in Lancashire, signed by its Abbot Roger Pyle, read: 'I, Roger, abbot of the monastery of Furness, knowing the misorder and evil life both unto God and our Prince of the brethren of the said monastery, in discharging of my conscience do freely and wholly surrender, give, and grant unto the King's Highness, and to his heirs and assigns for evermore, all such interest and title as I have had, have, or may have, of and in the said monastery of Furness, and of and in the lands, rents, possessions, revenues, services both spiritual and temporal, and of and in all goods and chattels and all other thing whatsoever it be, belonging or in any wise appertaining to the said monastery (155).' *Surrender of the larger monasteries*

The last of the larger monasteries were forcibly dissolved by an Act of Parliament in 1539 and most of their property was sold off. This is how the possessions of one monastery were disposed of in 1539: 'Sir Richard Ryche, Chancellor of the Court of Augmentations. Grant in fee of the manors of Magna Bursted, Westhouse, Whites, Gurneys, Bukwynes, Cowbrige and Chalwedon, Essex; the rectory and the advowson of the vicarage of Magna Bursted; and certain messuages, mills, lands, &c., in Magna Bursted, Parva Bursted Billerica, Gyngmountney, Mountneysyng, Hoton, Stok, Buttesbury, Laynedon, Nevendon, Lachendon, Bastildon, and Langdon, Essex; which premises belonged to the late monastery of Stradford Langthorne, Essex; and all possessions of Stratford Langthorne in the above named places, in as full manner as Wm. Huddelston, the late abbot, held the same (156).' *End of monasticism (1539)*

In 1537, Cranmer sent Cromwell a copy of the English version of the Bible known as *Matthew's Bible*, and urged him to get Henry's support for it: 'I pray you, my lord, that you will exhibit the book unto the King's highness, and to obtain of his grace, if you can, a licence that the same may sold and read of every person, without danger of any act, proclamation, or ordinance heretofore granted to the contrary, until such time that we the bishops shall set forth a better translation, which I think will not be till a day after dooms- *Cranmer urges an English Bible*

Henry VIII presented with a copy of *The Great Bible*

day. And if you continue to take such pains for the setting forth of God's word, as you do, although in the mean season you suffer some snubs and many slanders, lies, and reproaches for the same, yet one day he will requite altogether. And the same word as St John (saith) which shall judge every man at the last day, must needs shew favour to them that now do favour it (157).'

Henry agreed, and in 1538 he commanded every church to have an English Bible: 'Item, that you shall provide on this side the feast of Easter next coming, one book of the whole Bible of the largest

This engraving from *The Great Bible* shows Henry VIII delivering it to Cranmer (left) and Cromwell (right)

volume, in English and the same set up in some convenient place within the said church that you have cure of, whereas your parish-ioners may most commodiously resort to the same and read it; the charges of which book shall be rateably borne between you, the parson, and the parishioners aforesaid, that is to say, the one half by you, and the other half by them (158).'

Cranmer wrote a Preface to the edition known as the *Great Bible* of 1540, in which he said: 'Wherefore, in few words to comprehend the largeness and utility of the scripture, how it containeth fruitful instruction and erudition for every man; if any things be necessary to be learned, of the holy scripture we may learn it. If falsehood

Cranmer's preface to the English Bible

95

shall be reproved, thereof we may gather wherewithal. If any thing be to be corrected and amended, if there need any exhortation or consolation, of the scripture we may well learn: In the scriptures be the fat pastures of the soul; therein is no venomous meat, no unwholesome thing; they be the very dainty and pure feeding. He that is ignorant, shall find there what he should learn. He that is a perverse sinner, shall there find his damnation to make him to tremble for fear. He that laboureth to serve God, shall find there his glory, and the promissions of eternal life, exhorting him more diligently to labour. Herein may princes learn how to govern their subjects; subjects obedience, love and dread to their princes: husbands, how they should behave them unto their wives; how to educate their children and servants: and contrary the wives, children, and servants may know their duty to their husbands, parents and masters. Here may all manner of persons, men, women, young, old, learned, unlearned, rich, poor, priests, laymen, lords, ladies, officers, tenants, and mean men, virgins, wives, widows, lawyers, merchants, artificers, husbandmen, and all manner of persons, of what estate or condition soever they be, may in this book learn all things what they ought to believe, what they ought to do, and what they should not do, as well concerning Almighty God, as also concerning themselves and all other (159).'

Act of Six Articles (1539) Conservative in outlook, the Act of the Six Articles (1539) showed Henry's wish to keep a tight rein on Protestant doctrine. As head of Church and State, he did not want his supremacy threatened: 'First, that in the most blessed sacrament of the altar, by the strength and efficacy of Christ's mighty word, it being spoken by the priest, is present really, under the form of bread and wine, the natural body and blood of our Saviour Jesus Christ, conceived of the Virgin Mary; and that after the consecration there remaineth no substance of bread or wine, nor any other substance but the substance of Christ, God and man.

'Secondly, that communion in both kinds is not necessary *ad salutem*, by the law of God, to all persons; and that it is to be believed, and not doubted of, but that in the flesh under form of bread is the very blood, and with the blood under form of wine is the very flesh, as well apart as though they were both together.

96 'Thirdly, that priests after the order of priesthood received as

afore, may not marry by the law of God.

'Fourthly, that vows of chastity or widowhood, by man or woman made to God advisedly, ought to be observed by the law of God, and that it exempteth them from other liberties of Christian people, which without that they might enjoy.

'Fifthly, that it is meet and necessary that private masses be continued and admitted in this the King's English Church and Congregation, as whereby good Christian people, ordering themselves accordingly, do receive both godly and goodly consolations and benefits, and it is agreeable also to God's law.

'Sixthly, that auricular confession is expedient and necessary to be retained and continued, used and frequented in the Church of God (160).'

9 England: Protestantism, Reaction and Puritanism

IN Edward VI's reign (1547–53) Protestantism gained ground, notably in the English services of the Prayer Books. The differing demands of the two unsuccessful rebellions of 1549, however, still showed that the country was divided in its religious outlook. Under a Catholic monarch, Mary (1553–8), a Counter-Reformation was attempted, but it was resisted by the Protestants and became more and more unpopular. Elizabeth I's effort to establish a moderate Anglican Church, acceptable to all, was resisted by Roman Catholics and Puritans alike. It seemed religious conflict would never end. The Roman Catholics became a small minority in the country, but the Puritans attracted more and more support, and in the seventeenth century they were to show themselves determined to secure control of the Church.

Some chantries (endowments for priests to say masses for the dead) had been dissolved under Henry VIII. This Act, passed in the first year of Edward VI's reign, completed the dissolution: 'It is now ordained and enacted ... that all manner of colleges, free chapels, and chantries, having been or *in esse* within five years next before the first day of this present Parliament, which were not in actual and real possession of the said late King, nor in the actual and real possession of the King our Sovereign Lord that now is, nor excepted in the said former Act ... and all manors, lands, tenements, rents, tithes, pensions, portions, and other hereditaments and things above mentioned, belonging to them or any of them ... and also all annual rents, profits, and emoluments, at any time within five years next before the beginning of this present Parliament, employed, paid or bestowed towards or for the main-

Dissolution of the Chantries (1547)

99

tenance, supportation, or finding of any stipendiary priest, intended by any Act or writing to have continuance for ever, shall, by the authority of this present Parliament, immediately after the feast of Easter next coming, be adjudged and deemed, and also be, in the very actual and real possession and seisin of the King our Sovereign Lord, and his heirs and successors for ever (161).'

First Prayer
Book of
Edward VI
Two years later, an Act of Uniformity enforced English services upon the Church: 'That all and singular ministers in any cathedral or parish church or other place within this realm of England, Wales, Calais, and the marches of the same, or other the King's dominions, shall, from and after the feast of Pentecost next coming, be bound to say and use the Matins, Evensong, celebration of the Lord's Supper, commonly called the Mass, and administration of each of the sacraments, and all their common and open prayer, in such order and form as is mentioned in the said book, and none other or otherwise (162).'

This prayer from the English Book of Common Prayer prepared by Cranmer is an example of his mastery of English prose: 'Lighten our darkness, we beseech thee, O Lord; and by thy great mercy defend us from all perils and dangers of this night; for the love of thy only Son, our Saviour Jesus Christ. Amen (163).'

But there was much opposition to these reforms. One curate in Durham disapprovingly described the effect of the Act of Uniformity of 1549: 'The holy mass was utterly deposed throughout all this realm of England and other the King's dominions at the said Pentecost, and in place thereof a communion to be said in English without any elevation of Christ's body and blood under form of bread and wine, or adoration ... (164).'

Simple churchgoers must have found these violent changes very disturbing. A chronicler described what was done to the churches in Edward VI's reign: 'All images were pulled down through all England, and all the churches were white-limed and the commandments written on the walls. All the altars were pulled down. In every church all rood-screens were pulled down, and every speaker spoke against all images (165).'

Demands of
the Western
Rebels (1549)
Here are three items from a manifesto drawn up by rebels in Devon and Cornwall against religious change. They show how much people clung to the past for safety: '3. Item we will have the

masse in Latten, as was before, and celebrated by the Pryest wythoute any man or woman communycatyng wyth hym.

'4. Item we wyll have the Sacrement hange over the hyeyhe aulter, and there to be worshypped as it was wount to be, and they whiche will not thereto consent, we wyl have them dye lyke heretykes against the holy Catholyque fayth.

'5. Item we wyll have the Sacramet of the aulter but at Easter delyvered to the lay people, and then but in one kynde (166).'

The rebellion in Norfolk, led by Robert Kett, was, however, Protestant in its outlook; his demands included: '8. We pray that prests or vicars that be not able to preche and sett forth the woorde of god to hys parisheners may be thereby putt from hys benyfice, and the parisheners there to chose an other or else the pateron or lord of the towne.

Kett's demands (1549)

'15. [We pray that no] prest [shall be a chaplain] nor no other officer to eny man of honor or wyrshypp but only to be resydent uppon ther benefices whereby ther parysheners may be enstructed with the lawes of god (167).'

In 1552 another Prayer Book was introduced. It was more Protestant than the first, and the Act of Uniformity now compelled everyone to attend church every Sunday: 'From and after the feast of All Saints next coming [1 November, 1552], all and every person and persons inhabiting within this realm, or any other the King's Majesty's dominions, shall diligently and faithfully, having no lawful or reasonable excuse to be absent, endeavour themselves to resort to their parish church or chapel accustomed, or upon reasonable let [hindrance] thereof, to some usual place where common prayer and such service of God shall be used in such time of let, upon every Sunday, and other days ordained and used to be kept as holy-days (168).'

Second Prayer Book of Edward VI (1552)

During Edward's reign, the work of Church reform continued. Royal commissioners were sent to make lists of superfluous church wealth which was to be seized by the Crown. This is the list for the parish church of East Lutton in Yorkshire: 'First, one chalice of silver, taken away by Mr Wandisford. Item, one vestment of dornix, with all things belonging to the same, remaining in the hands of John Davisone. Item, 2 bells and the lead, taken away by Richard Mansfeld, deputy surveyor, by virtue of the late Act of Parliament. Item, the stones and wood, taken by the said Mansfeld (169).'

Seizure of Church goods (1552)

101

Overleaf (pages 102–3) Kett the Rebel seated under the famous "Oak of Reformation" issuing orders to his followers

MARI
MOST
E HENRI

DOVGHTER
VERTVOVS PRI
THE EIGHT

AGE OF

XXVIII YER

But when the Catholic Mary succeeded Edward on the throne (1553) the Reformation began to be dismantled. The preamble to the Act of 1553 passed by Mary's first Parliament, set out the reasons for repealing the laws passed under Edward VI: 'Forasmuch as by divers and several Acts hereafter mentioned, as well the divine service and good administration of the sacraments, as divers other matters of religion which we and our forefathers found in this Church of England, to us left by the authority of the Catholic Church, be partly altered and in some part taken from us, and in place thereof new things imagined and set forth by the said Acts, such as a few of singularity have of themselves devised, whereof hath ensued amongst us, in very short time, numbers of diverse and strange opinions and diversities of sects, and thereby grown great unquietness and much discord, to the great disturbance of the commonwealth of this realm, and in very short time like to grow to extreme peril and utter confusion of the same, unless some remedy be in that behalf provided, which thing all true, loving and obedient subjects ought and are bounden to foresee and provide, to the uttermost of their power (170).'

Mary's Parliament undoes the Reformation

Here are some extracts from various Injunctions issued by Mary, restoring the old religion still further: 'V Item, that every bishop, and all other persons aforesaid, do diligently travail for the repressing of heresies and notable crimes, especially in the clergy, duly correcting and punishing the same.

The old religion restored (1554)

'XI Item, that all and all manner of processions of the Church be used, frequented, and continued after the old order of the Church, in the Latin tongue.

'XII Item, that all such holy-days and fasting days be observed and kept, as was observed and kept in the latter time of King Henry VIII.

'XIII Item, that the laudable and honest ceremonies which were wont to be used, frequented, and observed in the Church, be also hereafter frequented, used and observed. (171).'

Under pressure from Mary, Parliament agreed to be reconciled to the Papacy: 'That we may as children repentant be received into the bosom and unity of Christ's Church, so as this noble realm with all the members thereof may in this unity and perfect obedience to the See Apostolic and Popes for the time being serve God and your

105

Facing page Queen Mary of England

Majesties to the furtherance and advancement of his honour and glory (172).'

Protestants
meet secretly
The Protestants were now completely driven underground. These were some adventures of a secret London congregation during the later years of Mary's reign, when heretics were being burnt at the stake: 'Betwixt Radcliffe and Rotherhithe, in a ship called Jesus Ship, twice or thrice they assembled, having there closely after their accustomed manner both sermon, prayer and communion; and yet, through the protection of the Lord, they returned, though

Silver-gilt medal of Mary I

not unespied, yet untaken ... But they never escaped more hardly, than once in Thames Street in the night-time, where the house being beset with enemies, yet, as the Lord would, they were delivered by the means of a mariner, who being at that present in the same company, and seeing no other way to avoid, plucked off his slops [loose trousers] and swam to the next boat, and so rowed the company over, using his shoes instead of oars ... (173).'

Burned at the
stake
Foxe wrote down the stirring conversation between the King's officer and a Protestant as he was taken to be burnt at Ipswich:

'Master Wingfield said to Kerby, "Remember the fire is hot, take heed of thine enterprise, that thou take no more upon thee, than thou shalt be able to perform. The terror is great, the pain will be extreme, and life is sweet. Better it were betimes to stick to mercy, while there is hope of life, than rashly to begin, and then to shrink." To whom Kerby answered, "Ah, Master Wingfield! be at my burning, and you shall say, there standeth a Christian soldier in the fire. For I know that fire and water, sword and all other things, are in the hands of God, and He will suffer no more to be laid upon us, than He will give us strength to bear." (174).'

In 1555 Simon Renard, the Spanish Ambassador in London, *Resentment* wrote home to Philip II, warning him how deeply Londoners were *in London* murmuring against the burning of Protestants: 'Sir: The people of this town of London are murmuring about the cruel enforcement of the recent acts of Parliament on heresy which has now begun, as shown publicly when a certain Rogers was burnt yesterday. Some of the onlookers wept, others prayed God to give them strength, perserverance, and patience to bear the pain and not to recant, others gathered the ashes and bones and wrapped them up in paper to preserve them, yet others threatening the bishops. The haste with which the bishops have proceeded in this matter may well cause a revolt. Although it may seem necessary to apply exemplary punishment during your Majesty's presence here and under your authority, and to do so before winter is over to intimidate others, I do not think it well that your Majesty should allow further executions to take place unless the reasons are overwhelmingly strong and the offences committed have been so scandalous as to render this course justifiable in the eyes of the people (175).'

A Catholic priest complained in 1556 to Edmund Bonner, Bishop *Protestants* of London, that nothing was being done about the Protestants in *in Colchester* Colchester: 'They assemble together upon the Sabbath day in the time of divine service, sometimes in one house, sometimes in another, and there keep their privy conventicles and schools of heresy … Your officers say … that the Council sent them not home without a great consideration. I pray God some of your officers prove not favourers of heretics. The rebels are stout in the town of Colchester. The ministers of the church are hemmed at in the open streets and called knaves. The blessed sacrament of the altar is blasphemed and railed upon in every house and tavern. Prayer and fasting are not regarded. Seditious talks and news are rife, both in town and country, in as ample and large manner as though there had no honourable lords and commissioners been sent for reformation thereof (176).'

Bishop Edmund Bonner of London

Cranmer the martyr   Cranmer had served in the Church in Edward's reign, as well as in Mary's. His conscience sorely troubled him. When he was first charged with heresy in Mary's reign (1556), he recanted, but in his last sermon before his execution he retracted all that he had written, and as he was burned at the stake he spoke bravely of his real feelings, holding his right hand in the flames: 'Now I come to the great thing that troubleth my conscience more than any other thing that ever I said or did in my life, and that is the setting abroad of writings contrary to the truth; which here I now renounce and refuse as things written by my hand contrary to the truth which I thought in my heart, and written for fear of death to save my life, if it might be. And, forasmuch as my hand offended in writing contrary to my heart, my hand therefore shall be the first punished; for if I come to the fire, it shall be the first burnt (177).'

108

Facing page. Above Archbishop Cranmer attacked for his beliefs, and *below* burned at the stake

The burning of the Archbiſhop of Canturbury, Doctor Tho

Foxe left an extremely moving record of what happened when seven men of Smithfield were burned at the stake: 'The proclamation with a loud voice was read to the people ... that no man should pray for them, or once speak a word unto them, etc. Master Bentham, the minister then of the congregation, not sparing for that, but as zeal and Christian charity moved him, and seeing the fire set to them, turning his eyes to the people, cried and said, "We know they are the people of God, and therefore we cannot choose but wish well to them, and say, God strengthen them!" With that all the people with a whole consent and one voice followed and said, "Amen, Amen!" The noise whereof was so great, and the cries thereof so many, that the officers could not tell what to say, or whom to accuse (178).' *Seven men of Smithfield*

On her accession, Queen Elizabeth I was very anxious to calm these terrible religious storms: 'Her highness doth charge and command, all manner of her subjects, as well those that be called to ministry in the Church as all others, that they do forbear to preach, or teach, or to give audience to any manner of doctrine or preaching other than to the Gospels and Epistles, commonly called the Gospel and Epistle of the day, and to the Ten Commandments in the vulgar tongue, without exposition or addition of any manner, sense, or meaning to be applied and added (179).' *Preaching forbidden (1558)*

Acts in 1559 restored the Royal Supremacy and the Second Prayer Book of Edward VI (with some changes). The Act of Unformity tried to prevent further changes in worship: 'Provided always, and be it enacted, that such ornaments of the church, and of the ministers thereof, shall be retained and be in use, as was in the Church of England, by authority of Parliament, in the second year of the reign of King Edward VI, until other order shall be therein taken by the authority of the queen's majesty, with the advice of her commissioners appointed and authorized, under the great seal of England, for causes ecclesiastical, or of the metropolitan of this realm (180).' *Act of Uniformity (1559)*

The Puritans, however, wished to hold their own services. Matthew Parker, Archbishop of Canterbury, issued rules for the clergy to obey, two of which are given here: 'Item, that they shall decently cover with carpet, silk, or other decent covering, and with a fair linen cloth (at the time of the ministration) the Communion *Parker instructs the clergy*

111

Table, and to set the Ten Commandments upon the east wall over the said table.

'Item, that all communicants do receive kneeling, and as is appointed by the laws of the realm and the queen's majesty's Injunctions ... (181).'

In 1569, the Earls of Northumberland and Westmorland led the 'Northern Rebellion', to rally northern England to the cause of Roman Catholicism. In their rallying speech they called on the armed support of all men between the age of sixteen and sixty. Would the violence never end?: 'Thomas, Earl of Northumberland and Charles, Earl of Westmorland, the Queens most trewe and lawful subjects, and to all her highness people, sendeth greeting:— Whereas diverse newe set up nobles about the Quenes Majestie,

Silver medallion of Elizabeth I

have and do dailie, not onlie go about to overthrow and put down the ancient nobilitie of this realme, but also have misused the Queens Majesties owne personne, and also have by the space of twelve years nowe past, set upp, and mayntayned a new found religion and heresie, contrarie to Gods word. For the amending and redressing whereof, divers foren powers doo purpose shortlie to invade thes realmes, which will be to our utter destruction, if we do not ourselves speedilie forfend the same. Wherefore we are now constreyned at this tyme to go aboute to amend and redress it ourselves, which if we should not do and forenners enter upon us we shold be all made slaves and bondsmen to them. These are therefore to will and require you, and every of you, being above the age of sixteen years and not sixty, as your dutie towards God doth bynde you, for the settinge forthe of his trewe and catholicke religion; and as you tender the commonwealth of your countrie, to come and resort unto us with all spede, with all such armour and furnyture as you, or any of you have. This fail you not herein, as you will answer the contrary at your perils. God save the Queen (182).'

The Commander of the Queen's forces anxiously reported from York that the rebels were very strong in the north: 'There are not ten gentlemen in all this country that favour her proceedings in the cause of religion. The common people are ignorant, superstitious, and altogether blinded with the old popish doctrine, and therefore so favour the cause which the rebels make the colour of their rebellion, that, though their persons be here with us, their hearts are with them (183).'

The Northern rebels gained moral support from Rome, for in 1570 Elizabeth was formally excommunicated for failing to support the old religion. Here is an extract from the Bull of Pope Pius V: 'Resting then upon the authority of him who has willed to place us (albeit unequal to such a burden) in this supreme throne of justice, we declare the aforesaid Elizabeth a heretic and an abettor of heretics, and those that cleave to her in the aforesaid matters to have incurred the sentence of anathema, and to be cut off from the unity of Christ's body (184).' *Elizabeth ex-communicated (1570) and 'dethroned'*

The same Bull also purported to deprive Elizabeth of the English throne and, more important, absolved her subjects of their obedience to her: 'And the nobles, subjects and peoples of the said realm, and all others who have taken an oath of any kind to her we declare to be absolved for ever from such oath and from all dues of dominion, fidelity and obedience, as by the authority of these presents we do so absolve them; and we deprive the said Elizabeth of her

113

pretended right to the realm and all other things aforesaid: and we enjoin and forbid all and several the nobles, etc. ... that they presume not to obey her and her admonitions, commands, and laws. All who disobey our command we involve in the same sentence of anathema (185).'

But Elizabeth was determined in these years to establish a truly national, Anglican Church, which would help unite her subjects. She felt that England must seek a national destiny, and as far as possible sever foreign connections. She meant to govern without the help of foreigners. So it was that in 1585 her Parliament passed an Act ordering the expulsion of Jesuits and Roman Catholic priests trained in seminaries on the Continent: 'All and every Jesuits, seminary priests, and other priests whatsoever made or ordained out of the realm of England or other her highness's dominions, or within any of her majesty's realms or dominions, by any authority, power, or jurisdiction derived, challenged, or pretended from the see of Rome, since the feast of the Nativity of St John Baptist in the first year of her highness's reign, shall within forty days next after the end of this present session of Parliament depart out of this realm of England, and out of all other her highness's realms and dominions, if the wind, weather, and passage shall serve for the same, or else so soon after the end of the said forty days as the wind, weather, and passage shall so serve ... (186).'

The Puritans, however, insisted that the Church needed further reform. This is an extract from a Puritan *Survey of the Ministry* for Essex made in 1586, which condemned the priesthood: 'Mr Ocklei, parson of Much Burstead, a gamester; Mr Durdent, vicar of Stebbing, a drunkard and a gamester and a very gross abuser of the Scriptures. Witnesses, Mr Denham, Mr Rogers, etc.; Mr Durden, parson of Mashbury, a careless man, a gamester, an alehouse haunter, a company keeper with drunkards and he himself sometimes drunk. Witnesses, Richard Reynolds, John Argent, etc.; Mr Cuckson, vicar of Linsell, unable to preach, he hath been a pilferer; Mr Wilkinson, vicar of Stansted, Mountfitchet, a gamester; Mr Fountaine of Much Brackstead, an alehouse haunter and gamester (187).'

But while Elizabeth sought to free her realm from Jesuit and other foreign religious influences, she was anxious not to let her Church fall under the opposite extreme—Puritanism. 'Uniformity' was her policy. In 1593 it became necessary to pass another Act of Parliament, this time forbidding the Puritans to hold their own church services. The Act said: 'If any person or persons which shall obstinately refuse to repair to some church, chapel, or usual place of common prayer, and shall forbear by the space of a month to hear divine service, as is aforesaid, shall after the said forty days, either of him or themselves, or by the motion, persuasion, enticement, or allurement of any other, willingly join, or be present at, any such

A Puritan family from a woodcut of 1563

assemblies, conventicles, or meetings, under colour or pretence of any such exercise of religion, contrary to the laws and statutes of this realm, as is aforesaid; that then every such person so offending as aforesaid, and being thereof lawfully convicted, shall be committed to prison, there to remain without bail or mainprise, until they shall conform and yield themselves to come to some church (188).'

Richard Baxter (1615–91) recounted how, as a boy, his father used to read the Bible to his family on Sundays, while the riotous games were played by the rest of the village: 'Many times my mind was in-clined to be among them, and sometimes I broke loose from con-science and joined with them; and the more I did it the more I was inclined to it. But when I heard them call my father Puritan it did much to cure me and alienate me from them; for I considered that my father's exercise of reading the Scripture was better than theirs, and would surely be better thought on by all men at the last; and I considered what it was for that he and others were thus derided (189).'

Why did the Puritans attract such a following? Thomas Fuller suggested a reason: 'What won them most repute was their ministers' painful preaching in populous places; it being observed in England that those who hold the helm of the pulpit always steer people's hearts as they please (190).'

Passing of the medieval world   The Puritans in England, like the Lutherans, Calvinists and Jesuits on the Continent, thought to bring men nearer to the knowledge and service of God as they saw it. Their search for reality and purity in religion shattered the unity of the great Christian Church of the Middle Ages, and destroyed the authority it had exercised over the minds of men for centuries. By the end of the sixteenth century Christians were separated from each other as never before, but there was arising already a new respect for the freedom of the individual conscience, and a new desire to discover the essential truths of Christianity which was to lead them into fresh ways of unity in our own times.

Glossary

ANATHEMA   A curse against God or the Church.

BEGUINE   The music or rhythm of a West Indian dance.

BENIGNITY   Kindliness.

CALVINISM   The theology of Calvin and his followers, stressing predestination and divine grace.

CHATTEL   A moveable possession.

CONVENTICLES   A secret meeting, especially of religious dissenters.

EDIFY   To benefit spiritually and improve oneself morally.

EMOLUMENT   A fee taken from a person's employment or salary.

ERUDITION   Being learned or showing great learning.

INCREMENT   An amount of profit or increase.

LITURGY   The forms of public services officially prescribed by a church.

OBLATION   A thing offered to a divine being.

PARSIMONY   Carefulness with money or resources – meanness or stinginess.

PENITENT   To be repentant of one's sins.

PONTIFF   The name given to a bishop, chief priest or the pope.

PRELATE   A person of high ecclesiastical dignitory.

REPROBATE   An unprincipled or immoral person.

SECULAR   Concerned with the affairs of this world, and not the spiritual or sacred.

SEDITION   Conduct or speech inciting to rebellion.

SEPULCHRE   A burial vault or cave, built into stone or made of stone or brick.

SIMONY   The buying or selling of ecclesiastical offices.
SPURIOUS   Not genuine – something which is not what it makes
   out to be.
SUFFRAGAN   A bishop appointed to assist a diocesan bishop.
SYNOD   The church council of senior clergy and officials.
TITHE   One tenth of annual produce of land or labour, formerly
   taken as tax for support of the clergy and the church.

Further Reading List

Reformation and Revolution, 1588–1660 by Ashton (Granada, 1985)

Reformation of the Sixteenth Century by Bainton (Beacon P., U.S., 1986)

Reformation of the Sixteenth Century in its Relation to Modern Thought and Knowledge by Beard (Greenwood Press, London, 1980)

Spotlight on the Reformation by Chris Gibb (Wayland, 1986)

Reform Thought in Sixteenth Century Italy by Gleason (Scholars P., U.S., 1981)

The Reformation: Change and Stability by Klassen (Forum P., U.S., 1982)

Reformation and the English People by Scarisbrick (Blackwell, 1984)

Picture Credits

Sources

(1) G. G. Coulton, *Life in the Middle Ages* (CUP, 4 vols, 1935),
     IV, pp. 360–1
(2) *Ibid*, I, p. 14
(3) *Ibid*, IV, p. 355
(4) *Ibid*, I, pp. 16–17
(5) *Ibid*, IV, p. 361
(6) *Ibid*, IV, p. 312
(7) *Ibid*, II, p. 146
(8) *Foxe's Book of Martyrs*, ed. W. G. Berry (RTS, n.d.), pp.
     94–5
(9) C. R. N. Routh, *They Saw It Happen in Europe 1450–1600*
     (Blackwell, 1965), p. 57
(10) *Ibid*, p. 90
(11) *Ibid*, p. 101
(12) Erasmus, *In Praise of Folly* (Allen & Unwin, 1915), p. 87
(13) L. W. Cowie, *Luther* (Weidenfeld & Nicolson, 1968), p. 115
(14) *Ibid*, p. 41
(15) *Ibid*, p. 38
(16) *Ibid*, pp. 41–2
(17) *Ibid*, p. 42
(18) J. Lecler, *Toleration and the Reformation*, trans. T. L. Westow
     (Longmans, 1960), p. 148
(19) *Ibid*, p. 150
(20) *Ibid*, p. 149
(21) *Ibid*, p. 149
(22) H. Bettenson, *Documents of the Christian Church* (World's
     Classics, 1943), p. 256

(23) B. J. Kidd, *Documents Illustrative of the Continental Reformation* (OUP, 1911), p. 19

(24) *Ibid*, p. 29

(25) Routh, *op. cit.*, p. 238

(26) *Ibid*, p. 239

(27) Bettenson, *op. cit.*, pp. 268–9

(28) R. H. Bainton, *Here I Stand* (Mentor Books), 1955), p. 87

(29) Bettenson, *op. cit.*, p. 271

(30) *Ibid*, pp. 282–3

(31) E. Armstrong, *Charles V* (2 vols, 1902), I, p. 77

(32) W. M. Conway, *Literary Remains of Albrecht Drürer* (CUP, 1889), p. 159

(33) Kidd, *op. cit.*, p. 89

(34) *Ibid*, p. 134

(35) A. G. Dickens & D. Carr, *The Reformation in England* (Arnold, 1967), p. 38

(36) Cowie, *op. cit.*, p. 73

(37) Kidd, *op. cit.*, p. 452

(38) Cowie, *op. cit.*, p. 77

(39) *Ibid*, p. 77

(40) *Ibid*, pp. 77–8

(41) Bettenson, *op. cit.*, pp. 287–8

(42) Cowie, *op. cit.*, p. 93

(43) Bettenson, *op. cit.*, p. 295

(44) Cowie, *op. cit.*, p. 89

(45) Bainton, *op. cit.*, p. 267

(46) Cowie, *op. cit.*, p. 96

(47) *Hymns Ancient and Modern Revised*, no. 183

(48) Cowie, *op. cit.*, p. 99

(49) *Ibid*, p. 110

(50) *Ibid*, pp. 111–12

(51) *Ibid*, p. 111

(52) J. R. Green, *Short History of the English People* (1876), p. 342

(53) J. M. Thompson, *Lectures on Foreign Policy* (OUP, 1924), p. 117

(54) Cowie, *op. cit.*, p. 115

(55) Bettenson, *op. cit.*, p. 301

(56) Routh, *op. cit.*, p. 267

(57) *Ibid.*, p. 267
(58) C. E. Jackson, *Huldreich Zwingli* (Putnam, 1901), p. 316
(59) *Ibid*, p. 316
(60) F. Wendal, *Calvin* (Collins, 1963), p. 21
(61) *Ibid*, pp. 38–9
(62) Routh, *op. cit.*, p. 278
(63) *Ibid*, pp. 272–3
(64) Bettenson, *op. cit.*, p. 298
(65) Lecler, *op. cit.*, p. 326
(66) *Ibid*, p. 329
(67) Wendal, *op. cit.*, p. 97
(68) Routh, *op. cit.*, p. 273
(69) *Ibid*, p. 274
(70) *Ibid*, p. 275
(71) *Ibid*, p. 275
(72) Wendal, *op. cit.*, p. 75
(73) Routh, *op. cit.*, p. 275
(74) Wendal, *op. cit.*, p. 75
(75) J. T. McNeill, *The History and Character of Calvinism* (1954), p. 178
(76) *Ibid*, p. 179
(77) Kidd, *op. cit.*, p. 329
(78) *Ibid*, p. 329
(79) *Ibid*, p. 329
(80) Thomas Platter, *Journal of a Younger Brother*, ed. & trans. S. Jennet (Fuller, 1963), p. 40
(81) *Ibid*, p. 40
(82) Routh, *op. cit.*, p. 322
(83) T. S. Whitehead, *Gaspard de Coligny* (1904), p. 37
(84) Lecler, *op. cit.*, p. 326
(85) Routh, *op. cit.*, p. 263
(86) *Ibid*, p. 327
(87) W. F. Reddaway, *Select Documents 1453–1714* (CUP, 1904), p. 94
(88) G. F. Young, *The Medici* (2 vols, 1907), II, p. 120
(89) N. L. Roelker, *The Paris of Henry of Navarre* (Harvard UP, 1958), p. 189
(90) *Ibid*, p. 238

(91) *Ibid*, p. 239
(92) Bettenson, *op. cit.*, pp. 302–3
(93) Roelkler, *op. cit.*, p. 295
(94) J. W. Burgon, *The Life and Times of St. Thomas Gresham* (2 vols, 1839), II, p. 138
(95) Routh, *op. cit.*, p. 229
(96) W. Harrison, *William the Silent* (1897), p. 23
(97) *Ibid*, p. 208
(98) *Ibid*, p. 209
(99) *Ibid*, p. 209
(100) J. L. Motley, *The Rise of the Dutch Republic* (1874), p. 804
(101) Routh, *op. cit.*, pp. 285–6
(102) *Ibid*, pp. 284–5
(103) *Ibid*, p. 285
(104) *Ibid*, p. 286
(105) *Ibid*, p. 285
(106) *Ibid*, p. 286
(107) Bettenson, *op. cit.*, p. 364
(108) *Ibid*, p. 361
(109) *Ibid*, p. 361
(110) James Broderick, *Saint Francis Xavier* (Doubleday, 1957), p. 63
(111) *Ibid*, pp. 74–5
(112) Bettenson, *op. cit.*, p. 365
(113) *Ibid*, p. 372
(114) A. Blunt, *Artistic Theory in Italy* (OUP, 1940), p. 108
(115) Bettenson, *op. cit.*, p. 373
(116) Platter, *op. cit.*, p. 207
(117) Reddaway, *op. cit.*, p. 74
(118) H. Gee & W. J. Hardy, *Documents Illustrative of English Church History* (Macmillan, 1896), p. 126
(119) *Ibid*, p. 127
(120) *Ibid*, p. 111
(121) Roger Lockyer, *Henry VII* (Longmans, 1968), p. 124
(122) Dickens & Carr, *op. cit.*, p. 26
(123) *Ibid*, p. 27
(124) *Ibid*, p. 15
(125) A. H. Thompson, *Visitations in the Diocese of Lincoln,*

1517–31, III, p. 83

(126) C. H. Williams, *English Historical Documents 1485–1558* (Eyre & Spottiswoode, 1967), p. 762

(127) Dickens & Carr, *op. cit.*, p. 28

(128) *Ibid*, p. 30

(129) *Ibid*, p. 30

(130) *Ibid*, pp. 42–3

(131) Williams, *op. cit.*, p. 678

(132) Dickens & Carr, *op. cit.*, p. 35

(133) *Ibid*, p. 37

(134) G. R. Elton, *The Tudor Constitution* (CUP, 1962), p. 322

(135) *Montaigne's Travel Journal*, trans, D. M. Frame (Hamish Hamilton, 1958), p. 949

(136) J. A. Symonds, *Age of the Despots* (1875), Appendix V

(137) Dickens & Carr, *op. cit.*, p. 20

(138) *Ibid*, p. 50

(139) *Ibid*, p. 51

(140) *Ibid*, p. 53

(141) *Ibid*, p. 57

(142) Williams, *op. cit.*, p. 719

(143) Dickens & Carr, *op. cit.*, p. 59

(144) *Ibid*, p. 67

(145) *Ibid*, p. 65

(146) Williams, *op. cit.*, p. 777

(147) Dickens & Carr, *op. cit.*, p. 72

(148) F. M. Powicke, *The Reformation in England* (OUP, 1961), p. 7

(149) Dickens & Carr, *op. cit.*, p. 95

(150) *Ibid*, p. 94

(151) *Ibid*, p. 98

(152) A. Fletcher, *Tudor Rebellions* (Longmans, 1968), p. 122

(153) *Ibid*, p. 124

(154) Dickens & Carr, *op. cit.*, p. 104

(155) *Ibid*, p. 104

(156) Williams, *op. cit.*, p. 788

(157) *Ibid.*, p. 825

(158) Dickens & Carr, *op. cit.*, p. 82

(159) Williams, *op. cit.*, p. 827

(160) Dickens & Carr, *op. cit.*, p. 110

(161) *Ibid*, pp. 128–9

(162) *Ibid*, p. 133

(163) *Book of Common Prayer*, Evensong, Third Collect

(164) Dickens & Carr, *op. cit.*, p. 141

(165) L. W. Cowie, *The Reformation* (Weidenfeld & Nicolson, 1967), p. 81

(166) Fletcher, *op. cit.*, p. 135

(167) *Ibid*, pp. 142–3

(168) Dickens & Carr, *op. cit.*, p. 138

(169) Williams, *op. cit.*, p. 791

(170) Dickens & Carr, *op. cit.*, p. 143

(171) *Ibid*, pp. 146–7

(172) *Ibid*, pp. 150–1

(173) *Ibid*, p. 158

(174) *Foxe's Book of Martyrs*, p. 390

(175) Williams, *op. cit.*, p. 839

(176) Dickens & Carr, *op. cit.*, pp. 161–2

(177) J. R. Green, *op. cit.*, p. 360

(178) Dickens & Carr, *op. cit.*, p. 159

(179) Gee & Hardy, *op. cit.*, p. 146

(180) *Ibid*, p. 466

(181) Bettenson, *op. cit.*, p. 338

(182) Fletcher, *op. cit.*, p. 150

(183) *Ibid*, p. 151

(184) Bettenson, *op. cit.*, p. 338

(185) *Ibid*, p. 339

(186) *Ibid*, p. 340

(187) Elton, *op. cit.*, p. 329

(188) Gee & Hardy, *op. cit.*, p. 493

(189) Richard Baxter, *Autobiography* (Everyman Edition, 1931), p. 6

(190) Thomas Fuller, *Church History*, quoted, L. W. Cowie, *op. cit.*, p. 87

Index

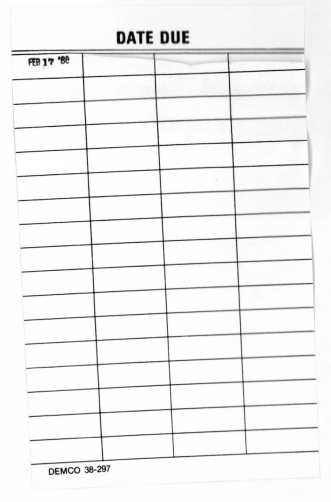

DATE DUE

FEB 17 '88			

DEMCO 38-297